Henry van de Velde

HENRY VAN DE VELDE

Klaus-Jürgen Sembach

With 320 illustrations, 10 in color

RIZZOLI
NEW YORK

Translated from the German by Michael Robinson

First published in the United States of America in 1989 by
Rizzoli International Publications, Inc.
300 Park Avenue South, New York, NY 10010

Copyright © 1989 by Verlag Gerd Hatje, Stuttgart

LC 87-42634
ISBN 0-8478-0858-0

Printed and bound in West Germany

Contents

Foreword

Some of the thoughts expressed here have been expressed by others before me, but numerous ideas have remained buried where they were originally published. It is not the intention of this book to test the foundations of Henry van de Velde's theses, nor yet to present a portrait of the man. Van de Velde does that much better in his own memoirs. They, and the biography by Karl Ernst Osthaus (1920), are now available again and may be read alongside this book. Many catalogues, including some quite recent ones, contain almost complete lists of the applied art created by van de Velde. A complete catalogue of his architectural work has just appeared, and a similar work on the furniture is in preparation. Even the painting of his early period has received due attention in several forms.

The object of this book is to detach the most important of the many facets presented by the artist van de Velde, the architectural *œuvre*, and to present it in sharp focus and without distractions. An attempt has been made to trace a creative line which, as van de Velde himself remarked, represents a force which owed its impetus solely to the person who felt it within himself. The intensity of van de Velde's belief in himself is truly moving, and still perceptible today.

Did none of his contemporaries surpass him? Yes and no. As far as real presence and virtuoso brilliance are concerned, Frank Lloyd Wright, Peter Behrens and Josef Hoffmann were certainly superior to him. However, in the complexity of his person, his ability to refract all facets of an epoch, he was on a different plane. This was a man who wanted almost everything, and therefore accepted that he could nowhere be complete. Van de Velde's life was characterized by changeability, and much remained transient. Nevertheless his *œuvre* is substantial, he never foundered.

Another factor strongly in his favour is that he made many comebacks. We have to set his great achievements from 1926 to 1936 alongside the high points he also reached between 1900 and 1914. Who has equalled that since? He was undoubtedly helped by the knowledge that everything created, including his own work, is only temporary. Van de Velde was tormented by this notion to good effect throughout his lifetime. In the end it seems to have made him very happy.

Memories of the wise old man on a little hill by a Swiss lake played their part in the writing of this book. There student and philosopher met across a gap of fifty years. This was the final period of van de Velde's life; he died, almost a century old, shortly after he had – as so often before – moved house: upheavals until the end.

He never lacked attention, even in his old age. As early as 1898 Julius Meier-Graefe, always keen to discover new talent, had devoted a whole issue of *Dekorative Kunst* to him, and thus opened up the road to Germany. It was a sign of unusual courage to invest so much in a completely unknown artist right at the beginning of a new movement. Karl Scheffler shrewdly followed in Meier-Graefe's footsteps, less enthusiastically but more consistently. Van de Velde's close friends also supported him in print: Harry Graf Kessler, Eberhard von

Bodenhausen and above all Karl Ernst Osthaus. Scheffler assessed van de Velde's position with extraordinary precision and insight as early as 1900: 'Wherever the ability to build in a new manner is found, one must sooner or later respond to necessity with beauty; and only an artist completely in harmony with his period can counter beauty with its *alter ego*, truth. Van de Velde is able to do this; and thus he has made himself first and foremost, and quite consciously, an artist of the age of railways, steamships and dynamos, the shining representative of the second stage of our development, which is moving forwards at the slow pace of historical reconvalescence, urging itself from pure line via applied art to architecture' (in *Die Zukunft*, December 1900). This indeed prefigured events.

Of the books which have appeared since van de Velde's death, Karl-Heinz Hüter's 1967 publication (*Henry van de Velde, sein Werk bis zum Ende seiner Tätigkeit in Deutschland*) was the first thorough examination of an important aspect of his work. This is a significant piece of research. A. M. Hammacher's book, which appeared in the same year (*De wereld van Henry van de Velde*), was more broadly based, but also less objective. It attempted to investigate the entire range of his persona and work. Léon Ploegaerts' and Pierre Puttemans' wide-ranging catalogue of his complete architectural output (*L'Œuvre Architectural de Henry van de Velde*), which appeared in 1987, is extremely painstaking, and very little could be added to it. The catalogue of furniture and related objects started by Wolf D. Pecher in 1981 is still in its very early stages (*Henry van de Velde, Das Gesamtwerk: Gestaltung*). Further contributions on the history of the Dutch periods can be found in the works of Günther Stamm and Salomon van Deventer. However, the most moving overall picture was given by the man who is the subject of it all. Van de Velde's memoirs are a miraculous creative achievement. The great exponent of *art parlant* finally surprised everyone with his ability to place himself at the centre of a work of this kind.

This book came into being as a result of the prompting, insight and patience of its publisher. I have come to know how much Gerd Hatje loves his work, and would like to thank Ruth Wurster and Anja Schliebitz for the care they took.

Klaus-Jürgen Sembach
February 1989

'Never in the course of a century has the name of an artist, even nowadays the name of Picasso, been spoken so often and so enthusiastically, so sceptically, with such lukewarm recognition or sharp rejection as that of Henry van de Velde. His ideas and demands must at the time have had the effect of high explosive. It was instructive to discover when studying books, polemics, essays and criticisms devoted to him, that people who are well disposed towards him, people not lacking in respect for his ideals, also have their objections. When, for example, Hamburg museum director Alfred Lichtwark found fault with van de Velde's silver cutlery, saying that it was simplified on the principle of a coal shovel, he was not aware what high praise this was. Coal shovels are known to be among the classically designed tools, like sickles, hammers, scythes and shears, that have retained unchanged both sovereign suitability for their intended purpose, and their neutral beauty. Max Liebermann liked the bubbling quality of van de Velde's mind very much, but rejected his highly individual furniture with the comment: "When I furnish my home, then I want to amuse myself. But not van de Velde."'

From the memoirs of the art dealer Eduard Plietzsch, published in the book *...heiter ist die Kunst*, 1955, quoted from *Henry van de Velde, 1863–1957*, Kunstgewerbemuseum, Zurich, 1958

7

Desk, 1899

An All-round Artist for All People

In his autobiography, Henry van de Velde presents himself as a figure of almost tragic dimensions, whose mission foundered on the conflict between ideal concepts and material reality. He sees this conflict as a determining factor in our society: it cannot be overlooked, but nevertheless is not inevitable. He complains about the incomprehension of an environment not prepared to take up his 'just and reasonable' ideas. The liberating force which informed his thoughts and creations should have been capable – he felt – of bringing about greater changes than he in fact achieved.

In making this remark van de Velde was less concerned with judgments of his work, which were in general favourable, but with its lasting effect. He saw his activities as transitory, aimed at a higher goal than the momentary satisfaction of his artistic ambitions. He did not intend the individual object to be important, but rather the doctrine that it represented.

Thoughts of this kind were not necessarily new – presumably every artist sees himself as leader of a school which will last for ever – but what is unusual is the force with which they are expressed. The lasting and not always comprehensible fascination aroused by van de Velde's work presumably results from this. First in his theories, then in his work, and finally also in his memoirs the artist demanded a degree of influence for himself which went beyond the norm. For him design was not restricted to the classical disciplines of architecture and craft, but extended to all spheres of human life, which was informed by it in absolute fashion. Outward harmony should be the expression of inner balance and considered form should reflect heightened awareness. Van de Velde consequently saw himself as the instructor of a civilization able to survive without self-deception and deceit.

His first and foremost ideal was the redemption of the modern world from its own ugliness. The dubious ersatz culture manifested in the historicism of the nineteenth century and created with the help of the machine – but not necessarily caused by it – was to be conquered by an approach to design that could be regarded as intelligent, genuine and original. Thus what van de Velde had in mind were artistic designs to be developed according to rules and not in arbitrary fashion.

The intention was not merely to conform to rules but to an inner logic. The spirit of the engineer was to determine all forms and elucidate the manner in which they had been carefully chosen. Structural honesty formed the basis, and all additions – including ornaments – were to confirm this principle. This functional quality, which might seem austere, was in fact handled in more complex fashion than the theoretical description suggests. It included a rhetorical element and left considerable room for artistic interpretation. Logic of design was seen as a *sine qua non*, but the degree and intensity of its realization were left open. Even fleeting consideration of his work shows that van de Velde interpreted this secondary principle in a most liberal manner.

The most important landmarks in Henry van de Velde's very eventful life were Antwerp, where he was born in 1863 and remained until he had completed his painting studies, then Paris and Barbizon. From 1885 he was back in Belgium, living in Brussels, then quietly in smaller places in the country. In 1895 he built a house for himself in Uccle near Brussels. In 1900/1 he was in Berlin, working very effectively as an interior designer. The German period continued from 1902 to 1917 in Weimar, where he had many good, if rarely epoch-making, contracts. A second vain attempt to establish himself successfully in Paris was made in 1910/11. In 1914 he built the theatre at the Werkbund exhibition in Cologne. In 1917 he was driven out of Germany by the war and until 1919 stayed in Switzerland with no great successes to his name. After that he committed himself to Holland for six years, but this also came to nothing. In 1926 he returned to Belgium and did a great deal of work in Brussels over the next ten years. In 1937/38 he built the Kröller-Müller museum in Holland. From 1947 to his death in 1957 van de Velde lived in a small town in Switzerland.

Henry van de Velde, *Geschichte meines Lebens*, edited and translated by Hans Curjel, Munich, 1962 (subsequently referred to as *Memoirs*)

Woodcut, *c.* 1895

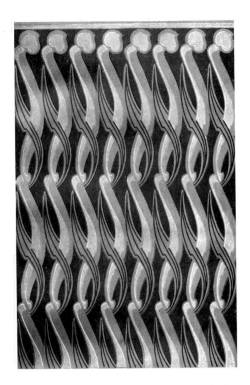

Wallpaper, 1895 (see also pages 22, 45 and 53)

Desk, page 8

Silver belt buckle, before 1900

A vivid example of this is the linear ornamentation which is a dominant feature of all the artist's early work. The basic principle is a dynamic that can be seen as the expression of internal currents of movement. The ornamentation pulsates perceptibly and has a force which – derived from the temperament of the designer – is able to communicate itself to the observer by suggestion, as if demonstrating the object's potential. At the same time – and this is in fact its primary function – it should mirror the structural context. To give an example: one of the best-known early pieces of furniture by van de Velde is the large kidney-shaped writing desk dating from 1899, which soon became the hallmark of the artist's work. Despite its wooden solidity it is completely broken up into bundles of lines, and makes a distinctly 'nervy' impression. It is bounded by energetically flowing movement which articulates its inner form and fills apparently dead areas with tension. Beautiful in a highly individual way, it always has greater significance than mere aesthetic balance. Every detail can also be explained in terms of purpose. The curve of the desk top corresponds to the outstretched arm of the user; the three-dimensional work on the rear edge serves both as a reinforcement and as a place for writing utensils. At points of concentration there are bases for screw-on candlesticks. Here, the dominant large-scale movement is accompanied by a more delicate paraphrase: a double band of brass curves from the foot of one candlestick to the other, forming a system of small bridges, and making the candlesticks, which could have seemed rather alien, an organic part of the desk.

A similar logic to that which informs the top of the desk also works for the front section. A single line encloses both the opening for the user's legs and the drawer sections. By this means structural coherence is vividly underlined, and the centre of the ornate structure emphasized. The clearly modelled relief has intrinsic value and is at the same time subordinate to the design as a whole.

The concave design of the outer ends is to be interpreted in two ways: as an ingenious space for books, and also as a vivid contrast to the solidity of adjacent sections. Formal and functional elements are consequently found in powerful symbiosis in this piece of furniture. Neither can be perceived as subordinate; they mutually enhance each other in dramatic fashion. This expresses the purpose of the piece of furniture in a highly individual manner – its character is not passive but active.

Rhetorical features play a large part. The intention is to show that objects should not just be useful, but should also make a recognizable statement of their usefulness. The desk asserts its quality as a desk in all its parts, in every aspect. Every detail works to demonstrate the heightened functionality which van de Velde sees as an ideal. He intends to captivate the user with curving shapes and swirling play of line, to place him completely under its spell. The piece of furniture confidently asserts how good and versatile it is.

This all goes to show that van de Velde was particularly concerned to be understood by as many people as possible; his work is intended to be 'comprehensible to the lay person' and to reveal itself without explanation. Certain missionary aims can be detected, and these led among other things to numerous publications. They were always pedagogic in content and intent, and aimed at restoring the modern world to health by means of a new beauty. Van de Velde saw himself as a Samaritan, with a precise knowledge of healing remedies.

The keynote was always an appeal to the power of reason. The essay 'Ein Kapitel über Entwurf und Bau moderner Möbel' appeared as early as 1897, in the de luxe magazine *Pan*, and is among the finest written by van de Velde. In it he states: 'The character of all my craft and ornamental work is derived from a single source: from reason, from reasonableness of being and appearance; this clearly also characterizes my privileged position and my strangeness. For I could not have found a better way of creating differently from others. Of course I set my sights a little higher; I am trying to find a new basis, on which we intend to create a new style; as the germ of this style I see before me one thing for which I must strive: to create nothing which has no reasonable grounds for existing. I also see a powerful means of realizing this: heavy industry, with its massive engineering plants, and their consequences.'

This key thesis is repeated towards the end of the article: 'Thus by the simple precept of being strictly logical, and by the inalienable principle of rejecting any design or ornament which cannot easily be manufactured and repeated by modern machinery, by making clear the fundamental organism of every piece of furniture and every object, and by constant attention to the ease with which it can be used, we arrive at a point at which we can completely regenerate the appearance of things.'

At the heart of this is van de Velde's credo. He never tired of varying and repeating it – in the course of which it becomes clear that the thesis remained a little general. However, the essay on the design and construction of modern furniture has the advantage, thanks to its restricted subject, of being more precise at two points: 'Now as far as furniture is concerned, the difference is as follows: a homogenous piece is preferable to a complex one, a homogenous room to an unordered, incoherent one. It must be recognized that every room has a principal focal point from which its life emanates and to which all other objects must relate and be subordinate. The various furnishings will be arranged in accordance with this newly discovered skeleton of the room, and thenceforth they will be perceived as the living organs of the room and indeed of the whole house.'

The words 'life', 'skeleton' and 'organ' show that van de Velde does not understand reason as an abstraction, but perceives it as a natural manifestation, based more on observation of available examples of logic than on a new intellectual structure.

The reason cited by van de Velde is also emphatically artistic, and directed at harmony: 'An individual piece of furniture only has unity if all the elements which could be described as alien, such as screws, hinges, locks, handles and hooks, do not remain self-sufficient, but are subsumed within it… otherwise we will not achieve the unity for which we strive above all other qualities; the symphony which is our ideal is vitiated by unarticulated or false notes.'

These elegant formulations were clearly not written for an inner circle, but directed at the large numbers of people whom his idealism strove to reach. It is easy to doubt today whether the populist line it expressed had a chance of succeeding. First it should be seen as what it primarily was: an attempt to win a larger community over to an artistic way of thinking. More people than ever before were to be given a sense of aesthetic values. At the same time, however, the process had to be mutual – the artist was looking for an understanding response, and the general public was to be helped by better design. The social component is unmistakable, and mirrors an attitude which had started to spread in the mid-nineteenth century. Its best-known representative was the English artist John Ruskin, whose strongly literary credo was reconstructed in more pragmatic fashion by his fellow-countryman William Morris.

The idea was to free the artist from the isolated position in which he found himself and to seek a new definition for his activity. It was suggested that this could be found in the socialization of all creative activity. Artists therefore changed from free to applied work, and created designs for model objects which then were manufactured in large quantities for the use of large numbers of people. Such action was noble and praiseworthy, but carried a contradiction within it – less in terms of the ideals involved than on the basis of previous experience. The desired result was indeed achieved, but at the same time called into question. For did not such procedures contrast with the premises of a characteristically unscrupulous industrial society, for which anything special was merely tolerated as part of the whole, but no longer a criterion by which things were measured?

Editor's office for the Paris periodical *L'Art décoratif*, probably 1898

Henry van de Velde, 'Ein Kapitel über Entwurf und Bau moderner Möbel', in *Pan*, 1897, issue 4

Packaging design, *c.* 1900

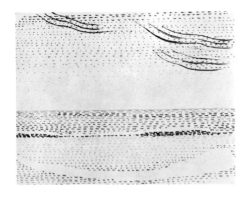

Sun on the Sea, 1888/89, black chalk on grey paper

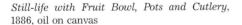

Still-life with Fruit Bowl, Pots and Cutlery, 1886, oil on canvas

The desire to ennoble the world artistically meant that a new awareness was called for, but this was opposed to the spirit of age, which valued economic expansion. The rapid development of the railways had caused an explosion in the volume of traffic and broken down barriers of time as well as space. At the same time industrial methods made it possible to copy 'history'. The spur to create something formally new disappeared as technical skills were perfected. It was not for nothing that historicism had become the appropriate style of the industrial age, clearly expressing the easy availability of both people and things. Given such dynamic perceptions it must have been tiresome to be reminded by aesthetic rules of areas of conscience which had been suppressed.

What could not be overlooked was that prevailing taste enjoyed the very things which artists found ugly. When Henry van de Velde announced his ideas for reform, intending to alter this state of affairs, he could not have suspected that they would to a large extent be fruitless. He spoke for them poetically and with moving zeal, and tried to give living proof of them in his own work. His eloquence was a driving force, expressed in deeds as well as words. He enjoyed using design as a means of agitation, and this often stimulated theory, rather than vice versa. Making points through creative work could easily be seen as more important than clarity of ideas. His intense faith still held scepticism at bay, and his firm conviction of being right and having moral legitimacy was unlikely to be shaken. Van de Velde was indeed a driving force, but he overlooked the fact that he could only bring about change in the aesthetic sphere. What he strived for beyond that had to remain a dream. The social effectiveness of his *œuvre* remained slight.

This resigned conclusion is generally in tune with the tendencies of the period; van de Velde's fate should consequently be seen in a broader context. His artistic contemporaries had similar experiences. Art Nouveau, the culmination of efforts at reform, had been beautiful but futile. Known in German as *Jugendstil*, 'youth style', it was not so much its youth which had made an impact, but rather its style, and its particular qualities had therefore been all the more successful. It lavishly confirmed the convictions of all those involved, at least for several years. But it also rapidly became clear that it had succeeded more in protecting artistic demands than in establishing new and real forms.

Presumably this could not have been otherwise, as the intention of changing society through artistic design was based on a false premise. Use was made not of objects designed artistically, but of objects which evolved from the task they had to perform, and which did not require a high degree of artistry; despite all honest affirmations of faith, little was done for the cause by the act of grace performed by artists entering the lowly plains of usefulness. It was inevitable that traditional standards and values should be applied to this largely new function. In the end, art was once more what was expected. However, this had its own demands, and basically did not permit 'application' on a broader scale. The apparently revolutionary process soon turned out to be restorative rather than anything else; it confirmed more than it changed.

This well-intentioned but basically mistaken movement had seemed – in its heyday around 1900 – like a redemptive force. It opened up prospects which must have seemed to bode extremely well, particularly for artists. Within a transformed society a position seemed to be emerging which would once more bring them meaningful involvement in life. The course followed by the young van de Velde is an almost perfect example of this search for fulfilment. After inclining towards music, in which he thought to have found himself, he then became convinced of his ability as a painter. He studied between 1881 and 1885 in his home town of Antwerp, and in Paris. He had access to the latest tendencies in European art and could train himself in everything which was fundamental at the time. From 1885 he lived alternately in Antwerp and the small fishing village of Wecheldersande. In Brussels he soon became involved with the enlightened group of artists, Les XX, which included Auguste Rodin and Georges Lemmen. Henry van de Velde not only exhibited his work, he also expressed himself in literary form on the position of modern art; his life seems to have been interesting and successful. As a painter he was capable of extraordinary virtuosity, and even his early pictures have an air of security and experience. But this phase of his life was to end in crisis, and bring him to the position described above. In 1892 he abandoned painting and turned to applied art.

This step can doubtless be interpreted in the way that van de Velde described it himself: as a moral decision. The artist no longer sees his activities as connected with the society in which he lives, and therefore looks for a different task. If we consider van de Velde's *œuvre* as a painter not just in terms of its quality – which is remarkable from the outset – but attempt to discern behind it the situation of its creator, then another interpretation is possible. His stay in Paris and the opportunities for artistic education afforded by Brussels were perhaps not entirely suited to the development of a reflective artist. Influences upon him were too various and too strong; they left him no room to look at anything else and prevented him from finding his own way. It is striking that van de Velde, in rapid succession and with a high degree of imaginative sympathy, reproduced the painting techniques of Monet, van Gogh, Manet and Renoir in his work. It was evidently not difficult for him to identify the characteristic features of these artists, take them up and reconstruct them. Often he hit upon the typical feature of his models better than they had done themselves. This perfection in adopting things is amazing and disquieting at the same time, because it suggests an ability which could never lead to fulfilment. Perhaps he felt himself to be an eclectic with an excessive capacity for sympathetic participation that inhibited his own work.

Henry van de Velde, *c.* 1890

A solution seemed to be emerging when van de Velde, first in 1887 and then even more importantly in 1889, encountered the pointillism of Seurat. The analytical nature of this painting technique reflected his own inclinations and forced him to a discipline which exceeded the virtuoso acquisition of formal methods. For the first time his sympathy was not just an adapting force, but took a thoughtful creative line within the meaning of the work: he created his own pointillism, as it were. He very logically chose simply built, largely two-dimensional motifs for this new technique. The picture *Blankenberghe* (1888) is a good example of this – anything concerned with detail and narrative has been relegated to the background, and the dominant feature is the contrast of light-coloured sand in the centre and dark shadows in the foreground. There are no half-tones to help us along the long stretch of sand, it is simply, glisteningly, there. For this reason the picture has great lucidity, and gives an impression of being almost insubstantial – as though one could pass through the canvas. Impressionistic flair is combined with a clear compositional technique, however, almost ruthless in its sharpness of focus. The shadows have a form that seems not to result from natural observation, but rather to have been preconceived. The broken outlines of houses, furniture and bathing apparatus, so often a feature in subsequent years, are already here in essence.

But there are also other elements and these contribute to the impression of latent violence. Thus the broad, gleaming central area creates expansive movement that almost explodes the balance of the picture. All other shapes are clearly in conflict with this one. The apparently peaceful scene is thus given a tension in contrast to our expectations of the subject. Sensations change, and instead of peace we sense an almost aggressive attitude. The sun-soaked beach is transformed before our eyes into an arena, a place where a belligerent incident is due to take place.

This picture was a key work in van de Velde's life. It was not only the acquisition of a new vividness which was decisive for him, but also the realization of the energy that could be released by an unusual method of composition. The libera-

Blankenberghe, 1888, oil on canvas △

Garden in Kalmthout, probably 1892, oil on canvas ▷

Title vignette for the magazine *Van Nu en Straks*, 1893 ▷

tion in this picture corresponded to a similar one in the painter's life. For years he had led a withdrawn existence in the country and finally had cared for his dying mother there. Now – in 1889 – he returned to society, as it were, and clearly stated his demands and aims. The new direction in his art – despite the natural subject which he had chosen – seemed urban and unsentimental, firmly opposed to any notion of an idyll.

The tension, sublimated and overshadowed by colourful refinement, which informs the *Blankenberghe* picture, reappears two years later in direct and undisguised form. The picture called *Garden in Kalmthout* probably painted in 1892, seems to be suffused with nervousness. Precise, academic pointillism has been replaced by short dabs of colour. The whole picture is filled with feverish movement, as though electrified. It rapidly becomes clear that the glow of a summer's day, a very strong feature, only serves to release an abstract play of movement, determined not so much by real objects as by galvanic principles of design. The picture does not seem hectic, however, as concentration is reasserted by the precise determination of all the lines. The anticipated disintegration does not occur.

This almost scientific concept of a work of art which attempts to show the laws which lie behind things inevitably led to an ever-increasing distance from realistic motifs. In the end these disappear almost completely. In van de Velde's well-known pastel, *Abstract Plant Composition,* of 1892/93 it is more the idea of a plant which is presented than the plant itself; and in some of the woodcuts of that period the stimulus is open to discussion.

Henry van de Velde turned his back on painting, despite the intensity of his results, probably less because he was dissatisfied with the independence of the results – as first presumed – but because he sensed that they were pointing him in other directions. The course upon which he had embarked was certainly rooted in painting, but its logical conclusion was translation into action rather than a dependency on individual sensations – it was urging him towards a legitimate application which was no longer 'free'. And for that, architecture and related disciplines were the only available means of expression.

The most visible sign of this attitude of mind was Bloemenwerf, the house which van de Velde built in 1895 for himself and his family in a quiet Brussels suburb. He designed every single detail himself, thus making the essentially modest architecture a statement of a particular kind. Though its appearance was innocently plain, it nevertheless offended the conventions of the period. Such a simple design was bound to cause confusion, and hints at a folk style can hardly have been an aid to communication. Over and above this, by doing what he did van de Velde had stated that the expert – the architect, in other words – was not in a position to fulfil the commission satisfactorily. He had set his own ideal, dilettante in the best sense, against the architect's specialized knowledge, or lack of it. The challenge could not be overlooked.

The house reflected a happy and relaxed way of life which seemed to offer a balance between isolation, which van de Velde had sought for a time in the country, and proximity to the capital, which he needed as an artist. It could have been the beginning of years of quiet happiness, filled with interesting work. But the idyll only lasted for a few years; it trickled away as a result of the extra work which it had called into being. It was quickly apparent there was to be no period of rest in this experimental course of events, that the process was only just starting, and was now making demands which had to be satisfied. Henry van de Velde had been discovered. First reports about the artist who operated so freely on the architectural plane appeared and drew him and his furniture designs, now numerous, into the spotlight. After this the isolation he sought could no longer be sustained, except at the price of cultural compromise.

His move to *nouveau-riche* but receptive Berlin, urged upon him by German friends, was the consequence of his artistic development. Around 1900 greater opportunities awaited van de Velde in Germany rather than in Belgium; he could assert his convictions much more effectively in the former country.

This led to the first real conflict in van de Velde's life. Whatever he decided had its negative side: had he stayed in Uccle he would for the sake of formal purity have had to betray the principles he had established, as his behaviour would have been considered too private and egotistical. On the other hand, his greater accessibility to the public at large would have brought with it external factors opposed to the spirit of his work: misunderstandings would have been inevitable. However, it would be wrong to over-dramatize the decision which had to be made. Presumably van de Velde did not find it too painful to go to Berlin, because his desire for publicity and broad effectiveness at the time carried more weight than the sacrifices of concentration and peace inevitably associated with it.

In fact there was a great deal to be said for this change of situation. Both social and rational aspects of his work predestined van de Velde to an unusual extent to exert influence in a way which crossed the boundaries of, yet linked, various fields. His theories and rhetorical formal language had to be generally comprehensible. They could be apprehended as an interpretation of modern technical civilization. The dynamic of his work made clear the technical impetus which increasingly influenced life. To this extent it communicated general experience and was not bound up with differing national views of art. It was particularly suited to expressing contemporary feeling.

Henry van de Velde's Belgian origins were scarcely a hindrance in this frontier-crossing operation; on the contrary, they provided a certain amount of freedom. As a representative of a country whose artistic physiognomy had turned out to be just as ill defined in the recent past as that of Wilhelmine Germany, he felt less oppressed in his new surroundings than an Englishman or a Frenchman might have done. And the Germans were indeed very receptive to him; there was inevitable curiosity about a man who had erected such firm theoretical support for his work. Van de Velde's eagerness constantly to declare himself an artist brought him increased trust. Both sides – the designer and his public – could weigh each other up in the hope of understanding each other.

His expectations were to a large extent confirmed in the spring of 1900. He was enthusiastically received in Germany, gained numerous commissions, and his theories were debated with interest. In his Berlin years he was once more the centre of artistic attention; some of his clients were highly respected members of society: François Haby, the court hairdresser, publishers Paul Cassirer and Ludwig Loeffler, art lover and industrialist Eberhard von Bodenhausen and finally Harry Graf Kessler, who was to be his most consistent patron. Karl Ernst Osthaus, a rich banker's son seeking a role in life, commissioned him to complete the Folkwang-Museum in Hagen in 1900, and van de Velde made this a truly exemplary design.

This last commission was particularly important. The designer must have been inspired by such suitable *données*: a feebly historicist, half-finished building, a patron with populist and educational aims, and his own mission-

'For Maria and me the most estimable thing about Berlin society was the enthusiasm with which non-German art and culture were greeted. In the field of music Berlioz' works were performed, and Bizet was very highly thought of. Hardly a day went by during our stay in Berlin when we didn't encounter a previously unknown work of considerable significance. Our horizons broadened more and more, and contact with contemporary art was a daily source of enrichment. In the early twentieth century a wind was blowing in Berlin which drove away the fog lying over the limited, conceited and ageing culture of the West. Maria and I were very happy.'
Memoirs, page 183

Three vignettes for the magazine *Van Nu en Straks*, 1893

Abstract Plant Composition, 1892/93, pastel

Dunescape with Sea, 1892/93,
pastel on pink paper

Angel Watch, 1893, tapestry in appliqué embroidery (see also page 54)

Reaper, 1891/92, lime-water colour on canvas

The Folkwang-Museum in Hagen, exterior, designed by the Berlin architect C. Gérard and built in 1899

Haby hairdressing salon, page 61
Havana Company, page 57

Showcase in the upper hall of the Folkwang-Museum in Hagen, 1901

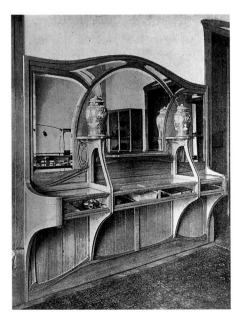

ary zeal. He was burning to confront outdated design with his new world of inner experience.

As well as its artistic character, the building was emphatically structural in orientation, and by no means unworldly. Iron banisters and visible steel girders introduced exposed engineering structures into a building associated with art. Such juxtapositions were still seen as a contradiction, and so this type of shocking gesture was to some extent held in check. On the other hand the design was less inhibited when interpreting technical necessity as well as displaying it. Sculptural cladding of steel girders, under which the profile of the load-bearing element could still be seen, was undoubtedly more attractive than presenting them unprotected, and poor proportions at the point of transition from iron column to wall arch inspired van de Velde to design particularly unusual stucco covering. Their abstract line embraced the unfortunate basic design of the original shell in highly imaginative fashion.

All this was taking place not in a secular building, but in a museum, and so the deed shone the more brightly. The Folkwang-Museum occupied a key place in architectural development, adding a nobility to Art Nouveau that it had not previously enjoyed. Now that the new style became a subject, rather than an object on display, it was freed from its rebellious attitude and took on a more permanent character. Things had unexpectedly and quickly come full circle – the reform movement, social in intentions but primarily aesthetic, had made an early entrance into the institution of the museum, signalling the end of its mission.

Numerous private commissions followed. Van de Velde's status as an artist was confirmed. Berlin developed a positively soft spot for him; it turned out that the parvenu among the capitals of Europe possessed a healthy measure of curiosity about its unusual newcomer. Added to this was the fact that numerous intellectual currents met in Berlin and created a mood of open-minded liberality, despite the city's apparent Wilhelmine austerity. The rich social life of the city, to which van de Velde was particularly attracted, meant that at times he was treated as a fashionable architect. This was not entirely unreasonable, as the commissions which brought him the most attention had indeed turned out to be spectacular: court hairdresser François Haby's salon (1901) and the Havana Company tobacco shop (1899). Both designs were brilliant demonstrations of the principles van de Velde claimed to have invented. The effect of these works could not be ignored, and they deserve praise beyond that merited by their absolute coherence of detail. The practice of filtering aesthetic effects out of technical necessity reached a peak in van de Velde's use of exposed pipework in his design for Haby. It goes without saying that the pipes were not just stripped of plaster and other coverings, they were also run in the most elegant fashion. Instead of being concealed, as was customary, they were practically celebrated. Such boldness was striking: not only was convention flouted, but van de Velde also surpassed the well-meant glossing-over which contemporary reformers of the calibre of Heinrich Vogeler or Otto Eckmann liked to feel was revolutionary.

Van de Velde had reached a peak of effectiveness within a short time, and could be permitted to feel that he and his theories were acknowledged. However, he seems quickly to have become aware of the dangers of producing such spectacular work. After only two years he answered a call to Weimar, where the Grand Duke resided, and moved to the small, highly tradition-conscious Thuringian town in 1902. Externally this seemed a continuation of the Uccle idyll, but the official position occupied by the artist *vis-à-vis* the court of the Grand Duke and old-established society had more of an effect on his life than at first supposed. His greatest support came from his friend Harry Graf Kessler, who had gone with him to Weimar and spread the word about him there. This was not without effect: some of van de Velde's best work dates from the early Weimar years. It shows clearly the vital ideal vision of their designer, based on material economy and intellectual flexibility. Theory and application are in

Picture gallery in the upper storey of the
Folkwang-Museum in Hagen, 1901

Entrance hall of the Folkwang-Museum with
Georges Minne's *Fountain with Boys*, 1901

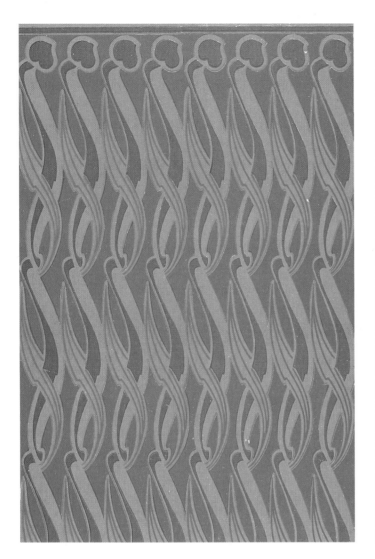

Wallpaper, 1895, often used in van de Velde's early interiors (see also pages 45 and 53)

'…and afterwards the colours still re-echo; they include a great deal of dark reddish-brown, deep, melancholy purple, serious shades of green, cool grey tones, subdued reds and the hard elegance of a white which sharpens all the modelling, combined with the heavy, matt glow of silver. The mood is at once cool and sultry.'
Karl Sheffler in *Kunst und Künstler* IX, 1910/11

Poster for the Tropon factory in Mülheim, 1897, lithograph (see also page 56)

Bedroom and dining-room in the Hohenhof in Hagen, 1907/8, recently reconstructed (see also page 143)

Dining-room for theatre director Curt von Mutzenbecher in Wiesbaden, probably 1906

extraordinarily close contact, and most things are characterized by spiritual functionality and polished form. This is particularly true of the tennis club which van de Velde built in 1906–8 in Chemnitz, of the high-gloss furniture, unusual for the time, and the cutlery, porcelain and lamps which he designed for local manufacturers. These objects combine Anglo-Saxon pragmatism with Romanesque elegance and show the poles between which van de Velde moved.

Although it is certainly true that the stimulus for his work came from England, his own inclination was towards France. He constantly tried to attract attention there, evidently seeing this country as the most suitable environment for him. As a man who spoke French as his first language and probably apprehended life in French fashion too, the artist must have believed, as convention required, that he should direct his energies towards the Mecca of his *métier*. Or did the attraction lie deeper than that?

In any case it must have been distressing for van de Velde that his Parisian début was a failure: the interiors exhibited there by the art dealer Samuel Bing in 1895 were much more admired in Germany two years later. The prejudices which had been expressed in Paris obviously did not apply here. The greatest disappointment was that the commission for the Théâtre des Champs-Elysées in Paris went in 1911 to the French architect Auguste Perret, despite van de Velde's involvement at the planning stage. This slight affected him deeply, but it was made up for in 1914 by the commission to build a theatre for the Cologne Werkbund exhibition. Other projects ended unhappily. An interior design for Victor and Natasha de Golubeff lost its point and was cancelled after Gabriele d'Annunzio abducted the lady of the house; the outbreak of the First World War prevented completion of a town house for the same patron. So France failed to respond to van de Velde's approaches and seemed unwilling to reciprocate his secret feelings for the country. Instead he was driven back to the German circles which he esteemed and respected for their receptivity, but which could never completely satisfy him. The experience of being a foreigner dependent upon German support was bound to become irksome after a time.

Certainly one must suspect that van de Velde over-reacted. Even the slightest setback led to verbose grumbling – particularly in letters. And he enjoyed complaining. He was always convinced that he was inhibited by external restrictions, and he knew how to paint a picture of himself as a man who had never really been able to develop his powers fully. This point of view is not unusual

24

Dining-room, shown at the 'Kunstgewerbe' exhibition in Dresden, 1906

among artists, but it is surprising in this case in view of undoubted successes to which van de Velde could point. In fact he had had no more difficulties to contend with than any other architect, and if one considers the didactic attacks that he was prone to launch, then his treatment in Germany had been remarkably generous. Respectful admiration was the order of the day; he even had a tame author, the talented Karl Scheffler.

One of his best works in this period was the Hohenhof in Hagen (1907/8). This villa was the second important commission which van de Velde had received from Karl Ernst Osthaus. The conditions were ideal and the architecture which emerged was clever and extremely thoughtful, a piece of work that was balanced in every respect. It was liberated to a large extent from customary convention, and superior to the villas that Peter Behrens, Bruno Paul and Hermann Muthesius were building in Germany at the time.

It was an achievement which could hardly be repeated in similar form. Van de Velde was forced to recognize that the period of individual commissions based on friendship and understanding was at an end. In the mean time he had definitely arrived, and received a correspondingly large number of offers, even though they were rather more conventional. Up until this point his work had consisted of sorties into the uncertain and the untried, supported by his patrons' faith that the highly esteemed, self-taught artist would master the task. Of course he did, and the very personal basis on which the work had been commissioned was undoubtedly a helpful factor. The trust with which he was surrounded must have touched van de Velde very deeply. As creative people often are, he was very dependent upon friendships. Essentially he lived through them.

A crisis now came about in which there was little others could do to help him. Harry Graf Kessler had been forced to withdraw from the Thuringian court because of a ridiculous incident, and houses designed for him, and other friends like Bodenhausen, Mutzenbecher and Osthaus, had long since been completed. Only van de Velde's patron in Hagen continued to be active, and introduced his relatives as new customers. Here close personal relationships retained their much-valued influence, but not as intensively as in the period when houses and furniture were still declarations of friendship. A slightly alien quality cannot now be overlooked.

Henry van de Velde also built a house for himself during this period. Hohe Pappeln, his villa in Weimar (1907/8), in many ways caught the mood of the

Hohenhof, pages 136–45
Mutzenbecher residence, page 108
Hohe Pappeln, pages 124, 129–35

Entrance to Theodor Springmann's villa in Hagen, 1914/15 (see also page 167)

Nietzsche stadium, pages 162–63

'…I very much regret that you have once more dropped your intention of drawing on the proportions of the Greek temple….

Your question seems very dangerous to me. I am far too fond of you not to feel compelled to point out a danger to which you seem oblivious. You speak of *l'effroi de l'abandon*. These are experiences which every artist has and which are the tragic element in his existence. But I cannot believe in complete loneliness, not even in the greatest of men. I could mention numerous examples. Where complete loneliness sets in, where the closest sympathizers and sharers in experience ultimately let one down, then contact is irredeemably broken and one can only move backwards or give oneself up to hopeless, sterile abandon. I remember the loneliest man of all, Nietzsche, whose significance was nullified at the moment when he lost contact with those closest to him and who believed that loneliness was his mission. No man, not even the greatest, can ultimately be alone, completely alone, without offending against world order and leading a fruitless sham of a life, a detached outsider.

You feel that I am dealing with quite general matters here and that all this has very little to do with your designing a Nietzsche temple. And you feel that it is real love which makes me say these words. Accept them with the same love and believe in the inner devotion of your faithful Eberhard.'

From a letter from Eberhard von Bodenhausen to van de Velde dating from 28 April 1912, quoted from *Eberhard von Bodenhausen, ein Leben für die Kunst und Wissenschaft*, Düsseldorf and Cologne, 1955

Erberhard von Bodenhausen combined a business career (including senior positions with Krupp and in the Tropon factory) and artistic interests in an unusual way. He sponsored the magazine *Pan*, and was a close friend of Henry van de Velde and Hugo von Hofmannsthal. He lived from 1868 to 1918.

Bloemenwerf house. It was certainly another attempt to find a place in which he personally could feel at home. The intimate interior of the study shows this no less clearly than does a family scene in the garden. Artistic credo and private happiness were intended to reflect one and the same view of life. But here too he was only to stay for a few years; moving into the house was again the pinnacle of a process of development which could subsequently only go downhill.

A contributory factor in all this was the fact that larger commissions with a truly liberating effect failed to materialize. This is true of the stadium in honour of Friedrich Nietzsche as well as the Théâtre des Champs-Elysées. The former project had been initiated by Harry Graf Kessler, following the awakening of a new Hellenism. The task must have been particularly suited to van de Velde's pedagogic inclinations.

But apparently both projects came too late. They turned out conspicuously puffed-up and overdecorated, and looked overloaded and lacking in concentration. We sense expectation too long stored up.

The crisis in this period was not contingent upon personal matters alone. The root of the problem was presumably much more a general ageing of the movement of which van de Velde had once been a leading figure than any direct frustration, such as uninteresting commissions or no commissions at all. Disillusionment with an artistic attitude which had been hailed as Messianic around 1900 had long since set in. A contemplative exercise like the foundation of the Deutscher Werkbund in 1907 is a good reflection of this. It was to place the romantic social utopias of the nineteenth century on an economically viable basis. Besides this, members of the Werkbund – artists, manufacturers and critics – professed loyalty to industry rather than craft as the basis of modern culture. This position was fundamentally intelligent, and should have had a considerable future, but it seems that the relevant ideas were not analysed methodically. The movement quickly took on academic form, and finally petrified into a new classicism. The rigidity of this was to a large extent interpreted as the highest form of truth – the misunderstanding was general, and almost all the artists of van de Velde's generation succumbed to it. It happened most clearly in the cases of Peter Behrens, Bruno Paul and Josef Hoffmann.

Van de Velde had only partially adapted to these developments and never really went along with this new turn of events. The baroque features of his designs in the last few years before the First World War were not genuine adapta-

Rest room at the 'Kunstgewerbe' exhibition in Dresden, 1897

tions, but served to conceal a new direction. The key lies elsewhere: too little attention has been paid to the fact that he was fundamentally influenced by Islamic architecture. An outward sign of this is the motif of the horse-shoe arch, which appears early in his work, and also his liking for abstract ornament. But much more revealing is van de Velde's inner affinity with the Orient.

This gives us a confusing and quite different view of Henry van de Velde – the rhapsodic rationalist is transformed into an oriental story-teller. This reversal of the familiar picture reveals some astonishing insights which, taken together, produce yet another. Van de Velde's particular rationality seems a confession of faith in a god who cannot be represented, but whose eye can be pleased by the logical interplay of forms. The abstractions within the artist's work evidently pay homage in this direction.

Once the eye is trained to this point of view then the apparently conventional interior of an elegant villa takes on features of a Moorish boudoir, in which a divan by a wall, apparently irregular corridors and alien arch designs combine in a new way. All at once, interior décor exists within a new climate.

We can now also understand the formal richness of van de Velde's major projects, their numerous corbels, shoulder pieces and curving roof designs. Of course the borrowing is never direct, the models cannot be precisely identified, but the spiritual relationship is evident. One of van de Velde's designs for the Nietzsche stadium in Weimar brings the Mameluk tombs near Cairo to mind, and individual façade studies for the Théâtre des Champs-Elysées in Paris are reminiscent of mosques. We can only speculate about the influence of van de Velde's journey to the Orient in 1903 at the invitation of shipowner Albert Ballin – presumably it only confirmed what had long been present in embryo: the tendency can be observed in the designer's earlier works. The rest room for the Dresden 'Kunstgewerbe' exhibition of 1897 is one of the earliest examples.

Although van den Velde's orientalism cannot be interpreted as direct historicism, it does connect the artist with one of the greatest sources of nineteenth-century aspiration. The artist, who sees himself as completely free, thus becomes part of a tradition, though certainly in an unusual way. This influence is essentially of an intellectual nature, and only partially takes concrete form. It is a sign of uncertainty that it occurs less clearly in the years after 1910.

Consequently we see here various circumstances pointing to the fact that van de Velde's work in Germany had reached a point of crisis, brought to an end by

Henry van de Velde, *Notizen von einer Reise nach Griechenland*, Weimar 1905

Ceiling light fitting, *c.* 1905

the outbreak of the First World War. But on this occasion too there was to be an elegant outcome. In 1914, of all years, van de Velde built his best building to date. The design for the Cologne Werkbund theatre, good both in itself and as an indication of the future, represented a new beginning, but it originated at a time when the ground was starting to give way.

The degree of confusion inherent in the situation can be illustrated by an episode in Weimar in 1914: German troops were waiting to be taken to the front by train, and van de Velde raced across the platform to them with a coffee jug. As always when he was excited he lapsed into French: *Du café, du café.*

We hold our breath for a moment because it is not possible immediately to grasp the complexity of the situation. This scene is a cruel and comic condensation of van de Velde's whole life, elucidating this often-homeless artist's entire existence as if by a flash of lightning: his idealistic zeal shuts out the realities of the world and invites scorn. The historical moment was doubtless stronger at the time than the individual in action, visibly contributing to his own misfortune. Could not van de Velde have presented this proof of his frontier-transcending affection in a way not open to misunderstanding? Why the wrong language at a moment of high tension? The failure cannot be overlooked and, as so often, this small incident hints at the truth.

The scene showed the artist as a human being, released from his official image. His action was evidently determined solely by the desire to be helpful, and this impulse made him throw caution to the winds. He went unprotected into an essentially emotional situation, which he thought would sweep him away too. Van de Velde had always wanted to reach a large audience, but up until now had moved only within the circle of his friends and a very few other connoisseurs. He had never become truly popular, and strictly speaking those around him had always drawn away from him rather than moving towards him. Thus it must have made him happy to overcome his isolation for a short time. On the station platform the communication which he had sought for so long was established. Artistic and social barriers seemed to collapse – an eloquent herald of a rational aesthetic was given the opportunity to make himself useful with an object from his own creative world.

Henry van de Velde's existence and the outbreak of the First World War in effect impinged upon each other in a particular way. The Cologne theatre had rehabilitated him as an artist, but before approval could become general the organizers were compelled by political events to close the exhibition. Van de Velde, who as a Belgian had at the time to cope with other restrictions, saw himself robbed of the experience of success – and thus the impression could be given that he was looking for a new audience on the station platform. But soldiers moving to the front were not an audience in a theatre, even if the festive uniforms might have given this false impression.

The station in Weimar was to be the site of van de Velde's farewell to Germany – he left for Switzerland in 1917. In summing up his Weimar period it must be said that the little Thuringian town so rich in tradition had seen within its narrow confines extraordinarily concentrated work by an artist functioning almost completely on his own, and whose demands on himself and his surroundings had been very high. Van de Velde had put his stamp upon a period of Weimar's history.

So what next? The commission to build a museum for the private art collection of the Dutch Kröller-Müller family – it reached van de Velde in 1919 – made amends for the absence of commissions. This seemed to be a chance to catch up on everything he had missed; the scope of the project and the money available were ideal, and seemed almost like a fairy-tale. At last external requirements were in tune with his own expectations of the task. If one considers the esoteric nature of the entire enterprise, its extravagant demands and the striking enthusiasm of Mme Kröller-Müller in particular, then the monstrosity of the

Werkbund theatre, pages 192–98
Hoenderloo museum, pages 172–77

design is not so surprising. It turned out to be merely ponderous, rather than large.

The detail of the building included many features which had been developed years before for the Théâtre des Champs-Elysées; neither can similarities with the Nietzsche stadium be overlooked. A new aspect, however, is the quasi-Egyptian massiveness, the lack of correspondence between internal function and external extravagance. Cyclopean walls were designed to enclose gigantic halls intended to contain only a few pictures. It constitutes a grotesque incident – what demon had entered the soul of an artist known to be prone to temptation, but also able to find aesthetic justifications?

The building was started but never completed because of financial losses due to German inflation. The idea that it could have been built, and indeed still be standing today, is horrifying. The vision is not easy to exorcise, because in the following years van de Velde had little to do other than design variations on the first idea and to draw all the necessary plans for the final version – down to the ventilation grilles for the central heating. It would still be possible to build the fortress-like museum exactly as conceived between 1921 and 1926.

Holland had brought van de Velde his biggest commission so far – but at the price of isolation. He was committed to the Kröller-Müllers as their private architect, built exclusively for them and made little or no public impact. He seemed to have been forgotten in both Belgium and Germany. However helpful the museum may have been for him financially, it had a disastrous effect on his work. It is obvious from the plans that they were drawn by a man out of touch with the developments of the day.

By 1925 it was clear that for the time being it was impossible to build the museum as planned. Even then the thought must have occurred that a smaller version was possible, and this was later built as the so-called transitional museum. It seems that the latter had a liberating effect on van de Velde, and from the heart of the colossus sprang the modest core. The massive chrysalis fell away, releasing clear, simple architecture.

The spark thus kindled burned very brightly from then on. Van de Velde became an architect directly involved in modern developments. From 1926 he was responsible for buildings among the best of their time. The transformation was strangely immediate, seeming to come from nothing – one day a disturbingly overblown design, the next work of extreme simplicity. External stimuli must have been involved, but they are not sufficient to explain why the transformation was so rapid and so thorough. Internal motivation is more illuminating: change had been coming for a long time, but van de Velde had hesitated to admit it to himself. It is inconceivable that he was unable to detach himself from the formal idiosyncrasies of the pre-war period because of scruples about all his work up to this point. Too much from that period seems to have remained incomplete, and to require apology. The spell was lifted at the moment when he ceased to be fixated on the huge museum. Van de Velde was able to turn away redeemed from a project which had mastered him more than he had mastered it.

Another contributory factor to this liberation was certainly the fact that in 1926 van de Velde had been officially recalled to Brussels, which he had left a quarter of a century before. The circle was completed, and his wanderings through Europe came to a temporary halt. Most of his late work was done in Belgium, even though what is probably the most mature product of this period, the Kröller-Müller museum, was built in 1937/38 in Holland. The change was also visible in the private sphere – the timber-built house De Tent, which van de Velde had built in 1920/21 for his stay in Holland, may have been a heavy-handed variation on Bloemenwerf, but the precise lines of his new house – his fourth, La Nouvelle Maison (1927) near Brussels, are no longer a reminder of it. It is a mixture of solidity and suppleness, austere without being dogmatic; the essential is carried out without agonizing. Contemporary work by Ludwig Mies van

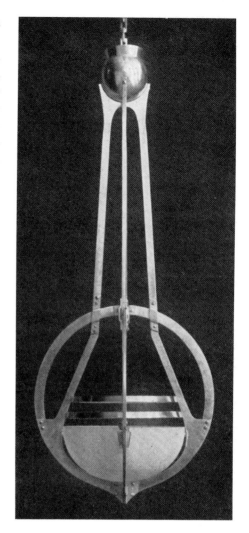

Ceiling light fitting, *c.* 1905

Cover design for Friedrich Nietzsche's *Ecce Homo*, 1908

der Rohe, Le Corbusier, J. J. P. Oud and Walter Gropius is certainly more complex, but also more rigorous. The subtle way in which van de Velde used three-dimensional features to blur the block-like basic form of his house is conciliatory when compared with the work of the above architects; it creates movement, transition and flux. His hand is recognizable in this characteristic, but it is now liberated from what previously had made it a rhetorical commentary. The principal insight which it gives us is that this coherence is not at odds with the individuality of the object.

Similar features can be examined more closely in the pavilion-like Kröller-Müller Rijksmuseum. This is an idea in the form of a building: its concentrated form not only suits its function to the highest degree, it also embodies its essence without waste. It is rare for architecture to be so collected and yet so confined to essentials.

Thus van de Velde's working life ended with a serene achievement; he was seventy-three years old when he built the museum. Physical strength to live through the process must have been as necessary as imaginative strength. Obviously he possessed the former to a high degree: he seems to have been little troubled by illness. In his youth he had been an almost fragile figure. He put on weight in Holland – another indication of his unhappiness at that time – but did not lose his agility; his movements and gestures remained spontaneous. His serious, narrow face, which easily acquired an expression of suffering, also filled out in that period, and his skull took on the massiveness of a cardinal's head. He cut an impressive figure, and scarcely anything reminded us that in the first half of his life his expression had always seemed somewhat harassed and nervy. In old age it was conspicuously relaxed.

The face which had matured with such conviction conveyed that one of the qualities which had helped to form it was perseverance. Only a high degree of steadfastness could have taken van de Velde through so long a period of creativity as his biography describes. The intellectual framework of principles which he had worked out for himself in his youth was complemented by a high self-esteem which enabled him to put forward theoretical matter in very lively form. The conviction that he was right created highly expressive objects almost automatically – at least in van de Velde's opinion. This did not preclude misgivings, but these were scarcely perceived by the public. Observers as a rule saw only the outward effect; on the other hand, there was a sense that van de Velde lived almost physically in his work. This is still the case today; even if we now feel that we can see mistakes here and there we are still affected, because we are touched by the passionate quality of the work.

Van de Velde never spared himself in the matter of explaining his motives. Not only that, he identified himself with each of his works just as wholeheartedly. In both matters he was engaged with unusual intensity. He always tried to reveal everything, his thoughts no less than the structure of the objects he created. This courage in declaring himself was moving, and attracted people to him, but could also act against him. It was not so much the fact that demand and fulfilment did not always correspond that his opponents reproached him with, but more their aversion to his presenting himself as a reflective artist. In this he took up a very modern position, which isolated him in many ways – for one thing he offended against conventional bourgeois notions regarding the behaviour of the artist, and for another he tended to reprove colleagues inclined to carry out their work rather more openly.

It was only when van de Velde abandoned the rhetorical dimension in his artistic reasoning, which was always aimed 'at everyone', and found an objective, almost egoistic faith in himself, that agreement and harmony were achieved. On the other hand, his original attitude expressed the self-doubt of the modern artist. This is clear if one recognizes that the almost Messianic euphoria of his beginnings is a sign of rebellion rather than of hope. The isolation which was a recurrent feature of his life necessitated outbursts which were a device for coping with his feeling of uselessness.

And yet his stated intention and reality could only have merged if he had curtailed his own demands and lost the expectation that he could be universally effective. The intellectual Europeanness which van de Velde attempted to embody was, despite favourable circumstances, only possible to a limited extent at this time, and was perhaps even – at least in the sphere of art – a mistake. Van de Velde presumably realized this during his Dutch period, when he finally had to accept that significance could not be forced into existence. Large gestures were less important than concentrated action. The road to this awareness was the moving force in van de Velde's work. It was a process of self-discovery, directed to some extent against his own nature, because the rational basis of his activity was for a long time overlaid with an expressive individuality which he took to be good for his life and work, but which in fact had an excessively dominant life of its own. Van de Velde's ideal way of dealing with this would have been the establishment of a theory of design with timeless laws. This would have redeemed everything, and created the discipline which he longed to see for both himself and mankind. His faith in reason as the primary basis for this legitimized the vision for him. However, it soon became clear that the rationality he cited was not general, but highly individual. In the last resort he was concerned with the aspect of the problem which affected him, and not the supposedly universal one.

The explicitly individual position which van de Velde originally took up also prevented him from forming a school. He did exert some influence over certain other artists around 1900 – Patriz Huber, for example, and Thilo Schoder, who had been his pupil in Weimar, was still working in a strongly imitative style even after 1920, but such things were trivial in comparison with the influence which he had hoped to exercise. At the very moment, however, when he could have founded a school he was either prevented by political events or in the shadow of other, younger artists. Time has blurred all this and left only a harmonious picture: the successful artist effectively at one with his environment. Enough of van de Velde's work has survived to create this impression. It is not false even if one looks only at the external, brilliant aspect of his work, but it must also be seen that this highly individual aesthetic charm was only possible because of an unusual spirituality of conception.

A résumé shows that van de Velde found effective goals and confirmation. Nevertheless, as an artist he was first and foremost a transitional figure, a transitory rather than a final manifestation. His searching is more characteristic than what he found. In my view everything material which he created points to the process which led to its form. This process is more important than the result, which must be considered temporary – this does not mean, however, that it cannot be complete, indeed perfect.

Transitions, positions repeatedly subjected to further development, were from the outset a determining factor in van de Velde's life – as much in his wanderings through Europe following offers of work as in his constantly changing spheres of activity he chose new ones on numerous occasions, because of social obligations or an artistic stimulus. His attitude was obviously also affected by the historical moment: the long-drawn-out transition from the nineteenth to the twentieth century, which was by no means as concise as its abbreviation to the formula 'around 1900' would nowadays suggest. Basically this process determined the whole of van de Velde's working life.

The way in which he saw himself as an 'artist-architect' also made him a transitional figure. He lived out an ideal between the epochs. After his early years he had been heading for a traditional artist's career, a direction which was soon to be transformed, but which never allowed its beginnings to be forgotten. From idealistic, rather romantic beginnings, he developed an increasingly prag-

Henry van de Velde in Oberägeri/Switzerland, the last place in which he lived, 1957

'He [van de Velde] was the intellectual temperament of the movement. His unduly narrow head and sharply drawn profile gave the impression that a Spaniard had stepped out of a picture by Velázquez; otherwise he had a southern slimness, and was mobile and had not a trace of stolidity. Although he had lived and worked in Germany for a long time he spoke broken German, but was able to express himself in an imaginative and trenchant way. Culture was not a word for him, but a reality, and even his inclination towards comfort and luxury seemed symbolic. The energy of his talent did not exclude elegance; where he was, the *petit bourgeois* was driven away, because he set his goals higher than anyone else. The style of living which hovered before his vision could have been called Greek-American.'
Karl Scheffler, *Die fetten und die mageren Jahre*, Munich, 1946, page 28

matic attitude, which finally enhanced his professionalism. His determination to show that he was an aesthetically trained engineer indicated that van de Velde was precisely aware where his future and the future of all architects lay. The vision was clear and in some phases he came very close to it. Nevertheless it was a long time before the impression faded that he was a talented dilettante, an artist not really at home in any camp. The unambiguity which the new age felt able to demand was something which he did not have, nor did he wish to acquire it.

His life was rich both intellectually and socially – he was not only very well read, but also knew many people in Belgium, Germany and France – and this justified his attitudes; he embodied an educational ideal of a complexity which would hardly be possible again. An architect who numbered writers, artists and art collectors among his friends, who knew how to come to terms with the world of the Thuringian court (he only seemed to avoid his fellow architects), was in this way a late representative of his discipline, unlikely to have successors.

It was inevitable that this personal dimension would – in the good as well as the bad sense – show up in his work. An obvious negative feature is the excessive number of pointers to significance, but a positive element was the belief, supported by theory, that he would be able to determine not only the form of objects but also reveal and make visible the actual 'idea' behind them. What was meant by this was the inner logic of a thing, the fundamental concept which would outlive formal transformation – the thought which had led to its birth. The inclination to abstraction which was a feature of his early work continued here in modified form. Naturally a demand of this kind went far beyond mere fulfilment of function.

Here again we can give examples: just as the pastel *Abstract Plant Composition* of 1892/93 demonstrated the 'idea' of a fruit as acquired by experience and not a copy of it, the famous kidney-shaped desk also rendered the 'idea' of a piece of furniture of this kind. Not that it is trying to be the ideal desk – presumably there was no such thing for van de Velde – but the special thing about it was that it embodied all the qualities and possibilities which could be associated with a desk. It is intended to transcend functionality to include thoughts which occur while seated at it, that is to say, the best thing that can happen there. As a theoretician and writer van de Velde was undoubtedly justified in risking this!

Henry van de Velde with Frau Esche at the upper garden gate of her villa in Chemnitz, probably 1903

Opening of the 'Künstlerbund' exhibition in the Grossherzogliches Museum in Weimar on 1 July 1906; Henry van de Velde third from the right

The same is true of small as well as larger objects. It can be as true of a teapot as of a piece of architecture. A buttress attempts to represent the idea of carrying, and a room embodies the idea of interior design in the meaningful disposition of all its elements. This omits the notion of ornament, which van de Velde pursued with particular passion. There are different degrees of convergence within the *œuvre*, but there is no doubt that his last building, the Kröller-Müller museum, begun 1937, represents a particularly flawless translation of the idea of artistic permanence.

Such a spiritual sense of one's actions, which now seems almost luxurious, made sense in the position in which van de Velde found himself. This situation gave him, changing and transitional as it was, the freedom to develop in almost any direction. He used this freedom logically, even though it meant that he completed few great works. The outcome was assessed differently and van de Velde was probably well aware that he was one of the last men likely to live through this kind of experience.

Henry van de Velde in the workshops of the Société anonyme van de Velde in Ixelles near Brussels, probably 1897

Freedom and Enterprise

Henry van de Velde found himself late. He worked as a painter for more than a decade, living quietly in the country. This was balanced by periods in Paris (1884/85 and 1887), Brussels and Antwerp. He was strongly influenced by Millet, Seurat and van Gogh: from Millet he took his ethical attitude; in the case of Seurat he was impressed by the planned nature of his technique, and the precision with which his colours were put together; and in van Gogh he found the line which was from then on to be sufficient expression of his temperament. Henceforth he saw the line as the dominant artistic medium. He never managed a personal meeting with van Gogh, but he saw pictures by him in an exhibition and in 1894 he saw pictures from the artist's estate at the house of his sister-in-law, Theo van Gogh's wife.

The change from fine to applied art constituted a social as well as an aesthetic protest in the late nineteenth century. Necessity – rebellion on the grounds of conscience – was combined with usefulness: a new field of artistic activity was opened up, or, more accurately, an old field was rediscovered and reclaimed. The process was not introverted, restricted to a new aesthetic for the few; rather it was extroverted directed at pragmatism connected with the public, and took into account the commercial conditions of the times.

There may have been another significant factor. After a period of intensive artistic activity dominated by Impressionism in painting and sculpture, by van Gogh and Cézanne – before new developments in fine art around 1910 – there came a period reserved, as it were, for architecture and related disciplines. Effort and interest switched at times – that was natural enough. Something else seemed about to take over, and sensitive observers were aware of this. Henry van de Velde was certainly one of them.

The person who provided the stimulus and ideas in this matter was the Englishman William Morris. Van de Velde endorsed him emphatically, praised him in public and became his prophet. However he saw him only – as was so often the case – as an artistic reformer and socially motivated entrepreneur, but not as a politician, which is what Morris had logically become. It was the fate of this great man to be only partially understood: as a designer or as a confessed socialist van de Velde must above all have been moved by Morris's work and way of life, and he copied these to a large extent. Not only did he turn to the design of useful objects, he also founded the Société anonyme van de Velde in Ixelles near Brussels, becoming an entrepreneur in his own right, and in the private sphere he designed and built a house for himself.

The latter decision had been encouraged by certain other events. In 1893 he had met Maria Sèthe, his future wife, and had clearly found a person clever enough to confirm him in his new direction. Many decisions, such as the move to Berlin, must have been supported by her – her mother was a German – and she may even have initiated them. It was the financial resources of her family which made it possible to build the house, as van de Velde had no means of his own. The

Henry van de Velde was born on 3 April 1863, the son of an Antwerp chemist. He spent a sheltered childhood as the youngest of eight children. After attending grammar school he studied painting from 1880 to 1883 at the Antwerp Academy of Art. In subsequent years he was much influenced by the latest French developments; in 1884/85 he lived in Paris and Barbizon. After that he returned to Belgium, with long stays particularly in the small fishing village of Wecheldersande, but at the same time maintained close connections with Antwerp artistic circles. In 1887 he stayed in Paris for a second time and studied a large Millet exhibition. From 1888 he was a member of Les XX, a group of Brussels artists, and became acquainted with Seurat's painting technique. In 1890 he first came across works by van Gogh. In this period he produced critical essays and lectures as well as his own pictures. The wall hanging *Angel Watch* dates from 1893, and in 1894 he married Maria Sèthe. In 1895 he built the Bloemenwerf house in Uccle near Brussels to his own plans. At the end of the same year he exhibited four rooms in the Paris 'Salon Art Nouveau'. He received his first contracts from Germany. In 1897 he took part in the 'Kunstgewerbe' exhibition in Dresden and founded the Société anonyme van de Velde with the help of Eberhard von Bodenhausen. In 1900 he moved to Berlin.

William Morris lived from 1834 to 1896 in England. He was one of the most versatile men of the nineteenth century – artist, craftsman and entrepreneur, but at the same time a writer and theoretician. He was for a long time close to the Pre-Raphaelites and throughout his life tried to realize John Ruskin's socio-Utopian ideas. To this end he co-founded in 1861 a firm to manufacture and sell model objects, which he took over completely in 1878. In 1883 he became a member of the Socialist League; in 1891 he founded the Kelmscott Press. Stylistically he inclined towards an idealized view of the Middle Ages.

Maria Sèthe, painted by Théo van Rysselberghe, 1891

Philip Webb, Red House in Bexleyheath/Kent,
built for William Morris in 1859

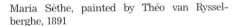
Van Nu en Straks, pages 15 and 17
Angel Watch, pages 19 and 54

The Bloemenwerf house in Uccle near Brussels,
1895

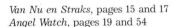

period in which he had been a painter, which he presented as a time of suffering, was now giving way to a new phase, which for the first time confirmed him in his ideas and brought him happiness.

Van de Velde had produced applied art before: decorated books, for example. The borders, vignettes and title pages which he had designed for the magazine *Van Nu en Straks* are often neither illustrative nor purely ornamental, but something in between. The degree of abstraction is surprisingly high and the internal vehemence, almost bursting out of the frame, seems to admit of no naturalistic detail. Even though the format is very small, they point to a sensibility on the point of eruption. The actual document of change is the well-known tapestry *Angel Watch*, designed by van de Velde in 1893. The high esteem in which this work is held is justified, now as then, for several reasons; it is important as a focus. Van de Velde had never previously used narrative, but had preferred static situations – landscapes, seated figures – whereas here he depicts a lively scene which additionally – this too is new – has a religious motivation.

Even more remarkable is the technique of execution. Van de Velde did not have the tapestry woven in the usual way; it was assembled from large pieces of material which were then sewn on to a backing with clearly visible stitches. This places areas and lines in a relationship of tension, and anticipates the principles by which he was to be guided on numerous subsequent occasions. This appliqué technique had the advantage of unifying structure and gesture, whereas if the usual weaving method had been used it would have got in the way of their diffuse and separate languages. This work thus not only represents van de Velde's transition from painter to designer, but also shows him to be a craft reformer. This made him a model successor to William Morris, but what made him artistically superior to the Englishman were the dynamic traits which he had been able to develop by traditional means on canvas, and which gave him greater boldness than Morris could ever have had at the time.

The long period of searching had not only allowed a new consciousness to mature within van de Velde, but had provided artistic experience which he could now transfer seamlessly to new spheres. The tapestry was still informed with van de Velde's painterly vision, but at the same time it contains a compressed indication of design possibilities to come.

Compared with the tapestry, van de Velde's own house, built a few years later in 1895, seems idyllic and withdrawn. Nevertheless it created a stir; despite its remote setting in a rural area near Brussels it became a Mecca for interested

visitors. It was seen by both Henri de Toulouse-Lautrec and Harry Graf Kessler; Karl Ernst Osthaus and Eberhard von Bodenhausen were finally won over to van de Velde here. His home was also the place in which the artist was to meet his most important supporters.

Van de Velde informs us that he designed his house himself, with advice from craftsmen. This makes him different from William Morris, who commissioned the architect Philip Webb to design his Red House in 1859. The ground plan of Bloemenwerf thus has some unmistakably dilettante characteristics. But if one ignores the details it is well suited to be the basis of a particular lifestyle – it is both innocent and charming. That could also be said of the exterior, although it is noticeable that the doors and windows are more securely arranged than the walls on the plan. The overall ideal for which he was striving is expressed at the heart of the house, the hall. The many doors and openings make it somewhat restless, but we can also imagine it as a linking area in which a young family could live. This model continued to be effective, and recurred in houses van de Velde built shortly afterwards: the Leuring house in Scheveningen (1902) and the Esche house in Chemnitz (1902/3). The spare, austere flights of stairs are very similar. Later this was to change: the stairs remained connected with the hall, but were allotted a space of their own. Thus Bloemenwerf was a successful model, and at the same time unique and unrepeatable. It could be the model for a view of architecture bound to tradition which saw progress as a moderate transformation of the known – as later represented in Germany by Heinrich Tessenow, Theodor Fischer and Paul Schmitthenner. It was an approach doomed to failure in the structural conditions of large modern cities, but at the time it seemed plausible. The example set by Bloemenwerf had an effect on many sunflower-surrounded houses on estates until the mid-twentieth century.

Thus the house did not represent 'new architecture', and despite the approval heaped upon it, van de Velde was soon made aware of this. He declined to repeat the experience. The garden façade of the Leuring house with all its random features did have a similarity with Bloemenwerf, but the street façade is much tighter. This is even more true in the Esche house, built shortly afterwards. It is uncertain whether his mother-in-law's little house near Bloemenwerf was merely rebuilt, or whether van de Velde was completely responsible for it. The polygonal form of the ground plan suggests that it was his work. In any case the design of the detail of the house shows van de Velde's hand. It demonstrates a rapid rejection of the two-dimensional style of his own house, which still seems

Garden side of the Leuring house in Scheveningen, 1902

Henry van de Velde on the stairs of the Bloemenwerf house, between 1895 and 1900

Bloemenwerf house, pages 41–45
Leuring house, page 87
Esche house, pages 80–82

The third house Henry van de Velde built for himself, De Tent in Wassenaar, Holland, 1920/21

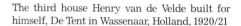

Maria van de Velde in the hall of the Bloemenwerf house; she is wearing one of the reform dresses which Henry van de Velde designed in large numbers at the time; in the background is her portrait by Théo van Rysselberghe, on the piano a score by Richard Wagner; between 1895 and 1900.

board-like and brittle. The moulded quality, of which van de Velde was master, was quick to come to the fore.

It is therefore justifiable to designate the short Bloemenwerf phase as 'Henry van de Velde *avant* Henry van de Velde'. It was a period which was still calm, solid, honest and upright, but also romantic and a little unworldly. It contains the seed of his future work, but the plant was not to resemble the seedling. He soon moved on from the style he had intended to be permanent: in five years van de Velde abandoned his rural idyll and moved to Berlin.

The prime motive for the move was certainly economic as well as artistic – the wish to be effective in a wider sphere. Again following the model of William Morris, van de Velde had set up workshops to build to his own designs, particularly of furniture, which he was now producing on a large scale. The picture which shows the artist among his craftsmen, carefully posed but none the less genuine, also shows that he was concerned to supervise the manufacture of his products. It is also clear that the furniture was made from very solid materials. The price was correspondingly high.

Van de Velde, with few exceptions, had received next to no response in Belgium, where in any case the modern movement was excellently represented by Victor Horta, who at the time was considerably more skilful; the former's only opportunity was abroad. France was his chosen goal, but the four interior designs which the art dealer Samuel Bing exhibited in Paris in 1895 elicited a divided response. The avant-garde element was probably recognized – this was the period that produced the notion of 'Yachting Style' – but it was seen as an affront to taste. It is not clear from contemporary pictures what in these interiors was designed by van de Velde and what was the work of the other artists involved. As was often the case in later years, he seems to have been inhibited rather than stimulated by working with others. The results are ambiguous and indecisive.

Germany, much less spoiled than Paris in such matters, reacted quite differently. Van de Velde received much recognition in Dresden in 1897 and in Munich in 1899, partly for the interiors which had been exhibited in Paris, and partly for more recent ones which bear his unmistakable stamp. This assured his future; now all the German patrons who discovered him had to do was to secure him commercially. It made no economic sense for the workshops in Belgium to continue; all commissions were now to be handled by the famous Hohenzollern

Dining-room, exhibited in Samuel Bing's 'Salon Art Nouveau' in Paris, December 1895

Exposition Bing
Je ne fais pas procès à l'idée de l'exposition, je le fais seulement à l'exposition du jour, d'aujourd'hui.
Quoi, ce pays qui a eu le coquet et rondissant mobilier de paresse du 18ᵉ siècle, est sous le menace de ce dur anguleux mobilier qui semble fait pour les membres frustes d'une humanité des cavernes et des lacustres. La France serait condamnée à des formes, comme couronnées dans un concours du laid, à des coupes de baies, de fenêtres, de dressoirs, emprunté aux hublots d'un navire, à des dossiers de canapés, de fauteuils, de chaises cherchant les rigides platitudes de feuilles de tôle, et recouverts d'étoffes où les oiseaux, couleur caca d'oie, volent sur le bleu pisseux d'un savonnage, à des toilettes et autres meubles, ayant une parenté avec les lavabos d'un dentiste, des environs de la Morgue.

House of Mme Sèthe, Henry van de Velde's mother-in-law, presumably built shortly after the Bloemenwerf house, which is close by

applied arts establishment in Berlin. This could not be sustained, however; manufacturing got out of control, and the workshop idea was sacrificed to industrial practices.

It was now clear that van de Velde was an economic as well as an artistic fact. The calculation was simple: as his reputation as an artist grew, so the number of commissions increased. It thus made sense for entrepreneurs to try to attach themselves to him. His upper-middle-class friends also saw his commercial potential, and did not encourage him solely from idealism. Two of them, Morton Graf Douglas and Eberhard von Bodenhausen, at that time heads of the newly founded Tropon factory – its product was a high-protein food – rapidly recognized the special visual appeal of his designs and therefore gave him commissions. It is not widely known today that as well as the famous poster, he was responsible for numerous other graphic works for Tropon, with a similarly spirited line.

His summons to Weimar in late 1901 had just such a speculative basis: van de Velde was attracted there by lucrative commissions. Officially he had been invited as artistic adviser to local craftsmen, but this label masks the actual intention. It is questionable whether van de Velde could work in this way – taste which has already been completely ruined is difficult to reform – but his presence did mean a large number of commissions for the craftsmen of Weimar, as well as confirmation of their technical skill and of course an enhanced reputation. Karl Ernst Osthaus also judged van de Velde in this way when he called him to Hagen. There is no doubt that economic motives lay behind the furtherance of modern art in other places, Darmstadt for example. Art Nouveau, at its climax in the crisis year 1900, was successful because it knew how to help itself through uncertain moments, artistically and of course artificially. Its aesthetic elements were important for as long as they could be used as a commercial stimulus – thus only temporarily. As soon as change came, the commercial stimulus disappeared. The rich years immediately before the First World War for this reason saw a new traditionalism in rather stiff clothing. This is not on its

Et le Parisien mangerait dans cette salle à manger, au milieu des ces panneaux en faux acajou, agrémentés de ces arabesques en poudre d'or, près de cette cheminée, jouant le chauffoir pour les serviettes d'un établissement de bains; et le Parisien coucherait dans cette chambre à coucher, entre ces deux chaises épouvantant le goût, dans ce lit, qui est un matelas posé sur une pierre tombale.

Vraiment, est-ce que nous serions dénationalisés, conquis moralement par une conquête pire que la guerre, en ce temps où il n'y a plus de place en France que pour la littérature moscovite, scandinave, italienne et peut-être bientôt portugaise, en ce temps où il semble aussi y avoir plus de place en France que pour ce mobilier anglo-saxon ou hollandais. Non, ça ce mobilier futur de la France, – non! non!

En sortant de cette exposition, comme je ne pouvais pas m'empêcher de répéter tout haut dans la rue: "Le délire…le délire de la laideur!" un jeune homme s'approchant de moi, me dit: "Vous me parlez, monsieur?"
Edmond de Goncourt, *Journal*, Paris, 10 December 1895, quoted from *Henry van de Velde, 1863–1957*, Kunstgewerbemuseum, Zurich, 1958

Secession exhibition, page 53
Tropon advertisement, pages 11, 22 and 56

'I could be prouder of the following principle, which is certainly individual: systematically to avoid everything concerned with furniture which could not be manufactured by *large-scale industry*. My ideal would be the reproduction of my creations by the thousand, though definitely under strict supervision, for I know from experience how quickly a model can lose its detail in production and, through all sorts of dishonest or uncomprehending manipulations, can seem just as ordinary as the object it is supposed to counter. I therefore expect to be thoroughly influential only from the moment at which a large engineering works allows me to make an effect according to the maxim that has given direction to my social beliefs: that a human being is worth all the more in proportion to the number of people to whom his life's work is useful, or whose lives are enhanced by it.'
'Ein Kapitel über Entwurf und Bau moderner Möbel', 1897

Holiday villa in Wartenberg, Bavaria, built by Henry van de Velde for the Weimar sculptor Richard Engelmann in 1913

own sufficient to explain the rapid decline of Art Nouveau, but it was certainly a determining factor.

Van de Velde acted shrewdly and presciently when he followed the particular laws of his existence and left Berlin, a lively and sparkling city, although it had spoiled him, to take up a position in Weimar which retained some of the idealistic Belgian beginnings. A smaller sphere of operation was more appropriate – as William Morris had also been forced to learn, good things were expensive, and could only be afforded by a limited, wealthy stratum of society. Van de Velde would presumably have found difficulty in reconciling with his aesthetic conscience a truly urban approach involving industry and mass production, of the kind that Peter Behrens had so wholeheartedly embraced; van de Velde was too scrupulous for that. If we consider it carefully, he had never really sought this position. It was part of his programme certainly, but wishing never to design anything 'of use to one individual only' was not meant to be a justification for mass production, but rather a doctrine: art, and therefore humanity, was to be healed by the example of his creations. Once this goal had been reached, manufacture would also have been more aesthetically ordered – at least, that was van de Velde's hope.

Advertisement for Henry van de Velde's firm in *L'Art décoratif*, 1898

The Bloemenwerf house in Uccle near Brussels, 1895

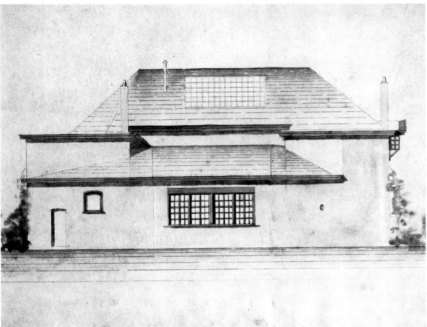

Drawings with watercolour of the front and rear

The Bloemenwerf House in Uccle, 1895

The house which Henry van de Velde built in 1895 in the Brussels suburb of Uccle while flirting with architecture is remarkably secure for a beginner. This effect is fundamentally strengthened by the fact that the street side is still symmetrical in organization; emphasis on the central section creates solidity and repose. But that is just about the only conventional point of the house.

Surprising features are its audacious simplicity, its combination of plainness and wit. The pinched outline of the gables makes a refreshing contrast with the clean, bright wall surfaces and the essentially worthy windows. The plasticity of the building gets under the guard of the modesty which was aimed for, and reveals the designer's artistic intentions. The design is ambivalent and ambiguous. A feature of van de Velde's being which was to become increasingly more important appears here for the first time in very reticent form.

Rural notions of design made a clear contribution to the shape of the house, but a detail as successful as the transition from central gable to porch roof can hardly be derived from this source. It betrays a structural sensitivity which is essentially independent. The curved base lines of the side gables also indicate a tension which is visibly trying to surpass the rural model.

The character of the house is thus not firmly established; it is neither farmhouse, suburban villa nor country residence. However, it does combine elements of all these building types in skilful fashion and synthesizes them surprisingly well. In doing this it also states the particular way of life for which the architect was striving. The house was a catalyst intended to link various levels of society. The result, however, was that the revolution which it in many ways represented also had traits which were bourgeois, and prone to preserve the bourgeoisie.

The securitiy of design shown in the exterior is not echoed in the interior. It is visibly helpless and gives the impression of having been built into the sculptural space of the building as an afterthought. Van de Velde's early predilection for much-broken outlines did create a successful overall shape, but highly unsuitable patterns for rooms were accepted for the sake of the chamfered corners. The principal room in the house, the central hall, which was lit from above, controls the outline in a most indistinct fashion, while a large drawing office threatens to explode the entire structure. A convincing design had yet to be found to connect life and work.

The house several years after it was built

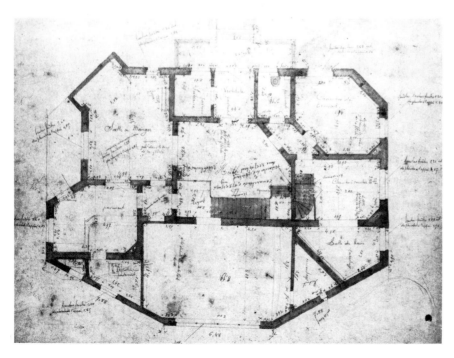

Sketch plan of the ground floor

Chairs from the dining-room

The Bloemenwerf House in Uccle, 1895

Henry van de Velde's favourite workplace was behind the large windows above the entrance, and formed part of the gallery which ran around the central hall. From here he had a view of the street as well as of the interior of the house, thus including the two poles between which he moved: the public – even if only to a limited extent – and his family.

The overall concept represented by Bloemenwerf demanded that the furniture should also be specially designed. The simple, informal interior made larger pieces superfluous, but tables and chairs enabled van de Velde to develop his ideas in model form. They were still free of ornamental embellishment and reflected the basic structural tendency with particular purity. Van de Velde rarely succeeded in expressing himself with such

austerity yet lightness as he did in the chairs for the Bloemenwerf dining-room. They are entirely functional, and their design springs largely from the logic of various carpentry joints. Their artistic tone arises from there and from there alone. It is true that this impression is only accurate within limits, but it communicates the idea behind the object very convincingly.

Even contradictions – such as the fact that the bars supporting the seats at the side give the impression that they are resting on the protruding transverse bar, although the latter does not really 'run through' – are not disturbing; the design is so pleasing that material correctness is outweighed. The extent to which the basic form can be varied is also captivating.

Study on the gallery above the entrance, overlooking the central two-storey hall on the right; in the background a printing press and poster by Toulouse-Lautrec; on the left-hand easel an abstract painting (probably by Henry van de Velde); between 1895 and 1900

The large drawing office on the ground floor of the Bloemenwerf house in Uccle near Brussels; on the right Maria van de Velde with a piece of embroidery of the kind used by Henry van de Velde to decorate reform clothes; between 1895 and 1900

Henry van de Velde in his home in Cranachstrasse in Weimar, probably 1903

Abstraction and Application

Henry van de Velde's own hint on how to understand his work is simple enough: 'A line is a force…' (*Kunstgewerbliche Laienpredigten*, 1902). All his early work is dominated by lines which make sinewy curves, bunched knots, or knots which encircle, supple and tight. Objects – first furniture and applied art objects, then later architectural features – are full of tight movements, on the surface as well as within the constructional framework. The principle proved transferable, and therefore of universal significance.

In van de Velde's work, however, a line is not simply a manifestation in one dimension, but is solid, in keeping with the power attributed to it. It always had volume: van de Velde's perceptions were never superficial, but always sculptural. In all he created moulding is a prominent feature, even when the line is confined to the plane of paper – in wallpaper, for example, it has such inner drive that it seems three-dimensional. Even van de Velde's earliest graphic work has such a vehement line that it is clear how the designer chafed against his restriction to a single plane. In the vignettes for the Flemish magazine *Van Nu en Straks*, movement is visibly forcing its way towards the observer, and advertisements designed a little later seem to be in relief.

It cannot be overlooked that this was a continuation of a characteristic of van de Velde's painting – a concealed or even overt dynamism which constantly seeks to burst through the framework. We have already discussed van de Velde's alienation from painting for moral reasons, and here we have a more formal one. In the long run work in one plane could never have satisfied him: he was essentially a sculptor, and always strove towards the third dimension.

In the early years van de Velde's hand clearly shows the influence of the art of the Far East. The foaming movement in borders, wallpaper patterns and designs for ornaments would seem to be derived from Japanese ideas. This is hardly surprising, as it would have been impossible for the young artist not to come across Japanese work in Brussels or in Paris – it was after all the great example for the entire era. But although he was following the trends of the period, his adaptations went far beyond what was customary in the late nineteenth century. He was looking for the structural law which lay behind the manifestation rather than an atmospheric effect. The motifs were still based in nature, and were not tested for mood value, but dissected into rhythmic forces. The approach was thus analytical in nature – an unusual procedure for the period.

An inclination to abstraction is also unmistakable. Van de Velde did not occupy himself with naturalistic models for long, but translated the ideas which they gave him into forms which have their own meaning and barely betray their origin. In the course of this, the grammalogue-like elements of the early woodcuts, which had still seemed improvised, were soon transposed into linear forms which continued to be informed with a certain legality. This is not deceptive, as van de Velde was indeed thinking of a grammar of ornament which would ex-

In 1900 he moved to Berlin, where he enjoyed a lavish social life and made public impact with lectures and essays. He formed a business connection with the Hohenzollern-Kunstgewerbehaus, which however was quickly dissolved. From 1898 to 1901 he had numerous spectacular commissions in Berlin: Kunstsalon Keller & Reiner, a reading-room for Bruno and Paul Cassirer, a sale-room for the Havana Company, the Haby hairdressing salon, and various private houses. In 1900/1 he designed the interior of the Folkwang-Museum in Hagen. In 1902 he moved to Weimar, having been commissioned to create an arts and crafts college for the training of Thuringian craftsmen.

Van Nu en Straks, pages 15 and 17

Woodcut for the title page of the volume of poetry *Salutations dont d'angéliques* by Max Elskamp, 1893

The Eiffel Tower in Paris, 1889

'A line is a force like all elemental forces; several connected but contradictory lines have the same effect as several elemental forces working against each other. This is an essential truth, and forms the basis of the new ornamentation, but is not its only principle. I have already on many occasions articulated the thought that we might soon discover complementary lines; but I will not require you to follow my hypotheses, and I only wish to explain here what absolutely must be admitted. If I now say that a line is a force, I am only asserting something which can be taken for granted: *it takes its force from the energy of the person who has drawn it*…. Nothing is lost, either of the energy or of the force, and an ornament thus designed, worked out according to the effect of elementary forces upon each other, attains the immutable formal purity of a proof and retains persisting force and effect for itself.'
Prinzipielle Erklärungen, from *Kunstgewerbliche Laienpredigten*, Leipzig, 1902

clude the arbitrary or random. One movement was supposed to respond to another logically and almost compulsively; mutual attraction and repulsion were to have meaningful, rhythmical logic; and negative space was just as important as positive drawing. If designs on one plane were still permitted a little freedom, van de Velde saw the relationship of ornamental form to spatial structures as strictly committed. They were to be tectonic and related to the structure of the object. Naturalistic motifs could thus hardly be suitable for such didactic organization of the decorative element. The abstraction introduced by van de Velde was thus in his eyes not an artistic end in itself, but a functional component of modern design as such.

The extent to which van de Velde's purely linear forms can be still be considered ornaments is questionable, but the effect is more important here than the definition. They went beyond classical ornaments and touched the observer in an unusually effective fashion. The reason for this is to be found in the second part of van de Velde's definition of himself which he gave in his postulate about line: 'it takes its force from the energy of the person who has drawn it.' Thus the artist established a direct connection with his work, which was a creation dependent upon him. This individual, almost egocentric claim was the expression of a great force, which should also touch those outside it, but it contradicted the entire instructive and rational basis which van de Velde demanded of all modern objects. Its anonymity, springing from a general logic, was difficult to reconcile with the signature of an artist who ascribed the power to live to the object alone.

This inner difference was among other things a question of scale. Throughout his life van de Velde had striven for large-scale design (even in cases when he had only a small scale at his disposal), and he did not abandon this even after some disappointments. It was obviously an expression of his temperament, and its impetus must have been with him from an early stage. As van de Velde was an educated man and far from naïve, he was also influenced by phenomena which lay outside the usual field of vision of young artists at the beginning of their career. He was stimulated not so much by the idyll of natural motifs and studio arrangement as by the dynamic of modern civilization.

In this respect Paris was a stimulating place. When van de Velde lived there – 1894/95 – the last French World Fair (1878) had been over for several years and the next was in preparation. Two of the most important buildings of the late nineteenth century were built for this event in 1889: the Eiffel Tower and the Galerie des Machines. Even though van de Velde did not see them complete he was in all probability able to follow the planning stages, and the disputes which grew up around the Eiffel Tower would also have reached his ears. An artistically sensitive person must have been struck by the debate, conducted largely in literary terms, about the supposed monster. It is unthinkable that van de Velde was not influenced by these testaments of the times, either during his stay in a Paris studio or in 1887, when he made shorter trips into town.

With hindsight we can assume that he was less interested in specimens of typical French taste than in those ingenious inventions which demonstrated technology in a form mastered by aesthetics. He presumably saw their constructional boldness as a prophecy which could give him the courage to see, beyond the predominating historicism, the beginnings of a new style.

Van de Velde – otherwise extremely communicative – only admitted these influences in a general way, and never in particular cases. He wrote: 'There is a kind of person from whom we shall not for long be able to withhold the title of artist. His work depends on the one hand on the use of materials, the applications of which were previously unknown; on the other hand, on a boldness which is so extraordinary that it exceeds the boldness of the builders of cathedrals. These artists, the creators of the new architecture, are the engineers' ('Die Rolle der Ingenieure in der modernen Architektur' in *Die Renaissance im*

Chair from the Bloemenwerf house, 1895

modernen Kunstgewerbe, Berlin, 1901). It is not immediately clear whether the expression 'title of artist' is the result of linguistic exuberance or whether it actually means what it says. If the latter is the case, then the engineers will have to accept the fact that they have been promoted and raised to new heights. Van de Velde is doing them a favour. The recognition he is giving them is influenced very much by his own position and is thus not without egotism: by declaring the engineers artists they are brought nearer to him, and he on the other hand has no need to apologize for his affinity to their work, which might have been considered a quasi-vulgar trait.

How did van de Velde occupy his own, still insecure, position and not be prevented from fulfilling his own demands? An analogy can be made with prose and verse: he wanted to set the more intimate mode of expression of functional design conscious of form, alongside the lapidary, sublime language of engineering. The former was to be spiritually similar to the latter and show related morality. In the Bloemenwerf house and his early furniture designs van de Velde had already come very close to this ideal of an everyday culture both disciplined and graceful. They were essentially honest, and the sincerity of the objects is undeniable. The simple chair from his own house shows a direct relationship with the Eiffel Tower. Six years after the tower was built van de Velde developed a structure which, in its soaring contours and richly articulated construction, is very close to the famous monument – obviously on a quite different scale. But what precisely is the significance of this? The relationship cannot be ignored, and it defines his intellectual position as closely as the creative sphere in which he wished to move around 1900 – and which he could permit himself to do as a dilettante!

The influence of modern railway construction is frequently clear in the work of Henry van de Velde, when he was using iron as a material – in banisters or lamps, for example – but more frequently in a transferred form. Most of the wooden constructions designed by him are informed by a tension similar to that

'The same laws which guide the work of an engineer also guide ornamentation, which I would like to place on an equal footing with technology in this work. The new architecture needs new ornamentation. The reflection and suppleness characteristic of the former must also be features of the latter.'
'Das neue Ornament', in *Die Renaissance im modernen Kunstgewerbe*, Berlin, 1901

For an exhaustive treatment of this topic see Eberhard von Bodenhausen, 'Van de Velde und die Eisenkonstruktion', *Innendekoration*, XIV, 1903

Title vignette for the volume *Dominical* by Max Elskamp, 1892

Theatre in Weimar, pages 85 and 89
Museum in Weimar, page 78
Esche house, pages 80–82

'Now as far as furniture is concerned, the difference is as follows: a homogenous piece is preferable to a complex one, a homogenous room to an unordered, incoherent one. It must be recognized that every room has a principal focal point from which its life emanates and to which all other objects must relate and be subordinate. The various furnishings will be arranged in accordance with this newly discovered skeleton of the room, and thenceforth they will be perceived as the living organs of the room and indeed of the whole house.'
'Ein Kapitel über Entwurf und Bau moderner Möbel', 1897

of steel. They seem to be curved and under pressure – but in fact they have been cut in curved lines from straight lengths of wood. The dynamics stem above all from the skilful reciprocal jointing of the sections, which form surprisingly three-dimensional, highly directed structures. This is the case with chairs, tables and cupboards and is even more noticeable in combinations involving walls or entire rooms. The relationship of such items with the frames of the hulls of large steel ships is evident immediately. In both cases the same dynamic forces seem to be at work.

This constructivist tendency determined van de Velde's early work as much as anything else, and is seen not only in iron and wood, but also in basket furniture. Here the curves are genuine rather than suggested, because of the elasticity of the material. Eventually the springy, structuring line is transferred to architecture – the first villas show this to the same extent as the early designs for large buildings (the theatre and museum in Weimar). It seems that the design principle is gradually transferred to architecture from furniture construction. Related details show that the path leads from small to large. The Esche house seems to have been 'carpentered' in the same way as a piece of furniture, and its projections are reminiscent of the cupboards van de Velde designed a little earlier. Again – and this is comparable with the relationship of chair and Eiffel Tower – the transference beyond the containing bounds of scale seems to have had nothing preposterous about it in van de Velde's eyes. It is apparently also possible in the opposite direction.

If the results are not always convincing, at least the procedure always demands respect. It revolutionized architecture from below, as it were – he did not think of filling in a previously conceived, integral shape, but of the creation and growth of form from constructional elements seen as generally valid, rather than specific. They were disposable over a broad range and thus no canon of application was needed. However, if forms could be transposed in this way, there was bound to be some uncertainty as to whether they had been correctly applied. Thus a process had been initiated which in fact could never end; however, it always included the notion that the idea was valuable, but its form not definitive. This 'incompleteness' is a particular feature of the early architectural designs, which clearly violate classical experience of immobility and statics. But the supposed deficiency is in fact an advantage.

The notion of organic growth was intentional; material was no longer seen as a dead element. 'The animation of material as a principle of beauty' is the title of one of van de Velde's most important essays on this topic (in *Essays*, Leipzig 1910). Houses, furniture and equipment are seen not as living but as 'lively' objects, possessing an inner potential for movement. The functional forces which van de Velde saw working within them were supposed to be not just purely physical manifestations, but also sensual ones. As we have seen from the example of the desk, his work could be capable of a kind of self-interpretation. For this to be possible a formal language was needed which was capable of transcending purely functional design, and thus, as it were, the realm of duty. In the realm of ornamentation van de Velde had quickly succeeded in finding inspired solutions, but the question arose of whether his ideas could be transferred to the whole. The attempt to prove they could was the pivot of his work.

It is therefore not surprising that the expressions 'organic' and 'organism' often occur in van de Velde's vocabulary. They were best suited to his ideas. However, things thus described should not be seen as quotations from life; the terms were used as an approximate designation for the fact that the things he was dealing with were 'reasonable' constructions with immanent expressive force. His further choice of words makes this clear: in his essay 'Ein Kapitel über Entwurf und Bau moderner Möbel' (in *Pan*, issue 4, 1897), van de Velde writes of the 'skeleton' of a room and obviously means by this the supple, space-embracing combination of all its elements into a functional whole. Once our attention has

Armchair, 1898, and sewing table, c. 1905

been drawn to the matter we discover that this affinity also applies to the details. The limb-like slender connections on the backs of chairs and table frames remind us indirectly of spokes, and the rise and fall of individual ornaments is similar to the formations of sinew and muscle. Nevertheless the treatment of such elements is always abstract, 'organic' being used in an associative sense and not as a naturalistic borrowing.

This aim for seemingly organic creations may also be the key to the fact that van de Velde's work, after the very slender, graceful formations of the initial period, became increasingly more powerful after 1900. The forms now have swellings, and are increasingly weighty. The ascetic 'iron' framework of the chair for his own house is replaced by more three-dimensional solutions in his later work. In their spatial evolution these are more lavish, seem less composed and flow more elegantly. Their sculptural value is indubitably greater. This is especially clear in the chair, which seems like a synthesis of the structure of pelvis and rib cage.

In van de Velde's eyes these forms obviously contained more power of artistic suggestion than anything he had previously created. It is therefore not surprising that they have the dramatic quality which was to increase throughout the course of his career. The lavish stucco of the museum hall which he showed in Dresden in 1906 was one of the first high points. The foaming theatricality of this building is far too eloquent for its relatively minor purpose; we sense mere husks intended to house rather slender content.

The limit of van de Velde's advance had been reached. The core was this, however: the new design was not to manifest itself in prosaic and indifferent guise, but to show lyrical and uplifting drive. Its outer glow – so the artist hoped – was to be a reflection of inner truth. Plainness alone would have been considered inexpressive. The statement made by a chair was not esteemed less than that of a large iron construction; both were equally important. But like any art form, van de Velde's had to overcome the temptation of becoming an end in itself and narcissistic. It was inclined to grow wordily insistent and excessively clear. The

Museum hall in Dresden, page 67

Titles of some texts by Henry van de Velde:
Eine Predigt an die Jugend, lecture, 1893; 'Was ich will', in *Die Zeit*, Vienna, 1901; *Kunstgewerbliche Laienpredigten*, Leipzig, 1902; 'Die verstandesmäßigen und folgerechten Konstruktionsprinzipien', in *Innendekoration* XIII, 1902.

'He is harmonious. Most geniuses are unintelligent, the massive demands placed on one eminent organ blunt the others. Van de Velde has the enormous gift of an extraordinary intellect. Quite certainly a great genius, the greatest in our movement, which is not saying very much, and certainly a phenomenon that will outlast time, which is saying more; but at the same time his intelligence is at least as great, and that occurs in isolated cases only. Others are instinctive, dreamer-geniuses, exceptional beings whom psychologists even classify as pathological; this man is perfectly self-aware. He is a man who is aware of his own enormous talent and has the abnormal will to exploit all the treasures of this store. This duality, which is the only thing which helps the applied artist to unity, is something which one will increasingly encounter in the work of van de Velde. One will constantly be surprised by the artist and at the same time struck over and over again by a reflection of such logical rigidity and consistency that even those who are not inclined towards modern taste and modern art are compelled to recognize it. Both are indivisible; even in the case of van de Velde's purely ornamental creations, apparently conceived with a completely free imagination, one is tempted to look for a logical proof; we will see that this is indeed available.'
Julius Meier-Graefe, 'Henry van de Velde', in the magazine *Dekorative Kunst*, III, 1898/99

rhetorical traits cannot be overlooked – van de Velde was probably more linguistically gifted than any other late nineteenth-century artist, in the literal and the formally figurative sense. However, this too contained a danger.

The unusually large number of texts written by him support this assertion, but are essentially unnecessary to make it clear that he liked to see his houses, furniture, silver and – last but not least – book bindings as a kind of *art parlant*. As in the example of the large writing desk, these objects did not just fulfil a function, they also elucidated it: the whole appearance of an object attempted to express its meaning and purpose in eye-catching fashion. This 'art of persuasion' was not just practised in words of van de Velde's own invention. They had content and meaning which were not only new and unusual, but also demanding. Despite their claim to be 'comprehensible to the lay person' van de Velde's works presupposed particular empathy; they demanded that the observer be sensitive and educated enough to understand them.

Thus there was a limitation of effectiveness which stemmed directly from the person of the artist, and the cause was in his character and background. Thanks to the traditional education which he had received almost as a matter of course in his parents' house, and his studies abroad, but above all because of his long-delayed entry into an active and involved life, van de Velde had been able to develop into a well-read and reflective artist. He was an educated man in the classical sense. Everything he did was marked by the need to be knowing, informed and eloquent. He was thus a representative of that contradictory type, the bourgeois revolutionary, whose tragic fate it was that his attitude contradicted much of what he thought, said and did. Without his comprehensive education he would have been impossible as a phenomenon, but at the same time it was a hindrance to him: particularly before 1900 he can be seen to know too much. Most of the objects created by van de Velde are stimulating and intelligent, but they are too complex to have that directness which really has the power to change. His activities could therefore be seen as the artful quotation of a concept, and not as the application of it.

Vignette from *Dekorative Kunst*, III, 1898/99; the flow of its lines seems to reflect that of the desk opposite

Study, shown at the Secession exhibition in Munich, 1899 (the desk is shown on page 8)

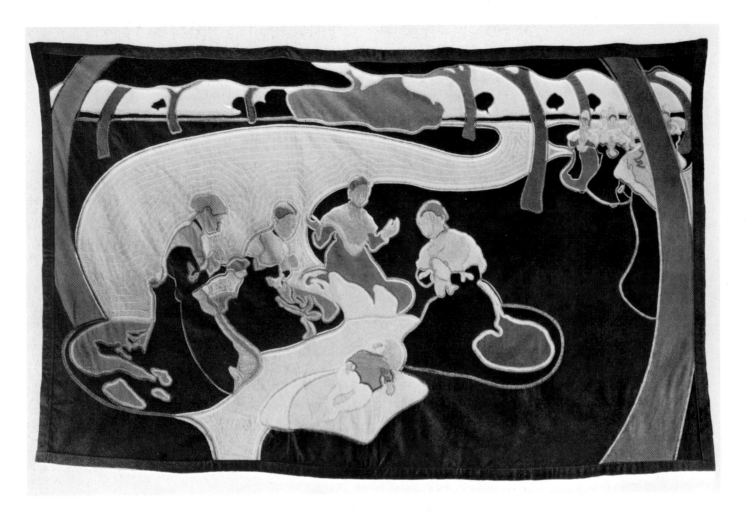

Angel Watch, 1893, tapestry (see also page 19)

Dynamic Forces

The sweeping, tension-filled line characteristic of Henry van de Velde's early interior designs had already featured in his pictures. The tapestry *Angel Watch* is a key work here, as it was van de Velde's first in the field of applied art. The scene which gives the work its title is still represented figuratively, but the way in which the surrounding landscape is portrayed is subject to other laws. The bending trees and sweep of the path can be seen as a framing design which, simplified to the extent that it is here, articulates rather than illustrates. Nature is transformed into spatial and dynamic form.

The numerous curves which van de Velde so often used in his early interiors seem to have been borrowed directly from the tapestry, and like the trees surrounding the biblical scene, they are markedly expressive in effect, contained within frames which they constantly threaten to burst. They are irregular, the outlines being composed of segments curved in different ways. Repetitions create a strong rhythm, which makes the room seem dynamically agitated rather than static.

These two rooms were among van de Velde's first works in the field of applied art, which was new to him at the time. Directly after changing from painting to interior design he created numerous interiors, all similar in form. Their elements were, however, treated 'uneconomically'; despite a formal relationship their unity was additive, not structural, as it did not provide sufficient separation between the structure of the room and the accompanying forms.

The frieze and mosaic in the smoking-room were designed by the Belgian artist Georges Lemmen.

Smoking-room, exhibited at the 'Salon Art Nouveau' in Paris, 1895

Interior for Léon Biart, Brussels, 1896/97

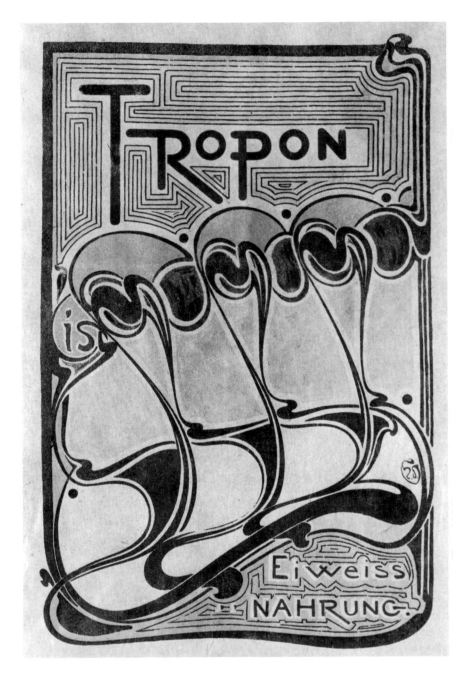

Poster for the Tropon factory, 1897 (see also page 22)

The Function of Line

In the poster, naturalistic elements of the kind featured in the scene with figures in the tapestry *Angel Watch* have taken on an abstract life of their own. The interplay of lines is primarily graphically attractive, but can also be seen as an expression of energy, and as such is correct for the poster, which is a food advertisement.

All the elements characteristic of van de Velde's handling of line appear in this poster: rapid double change of direction, dramatized by swelling, the interplay of alternate soft and tense movement, and finally the considered relationship into which the lines are set with the surfaces around which they play. The poster also shows how linear forms tend to detach themselves from the surface. Immediate transfer to the spatial is then possible.

The interior of the Havana Company saleroom combines linear and spatial elements in a very disciplined manner. The whole design is characterized by a logical synthesis of two- and three-dimensional linear structures. On each occasion a structural idea can be identified. Thus the painted frieze supports the ceiling and integrates the differing heights of doorway arches and shelf units. As well as a formative function it has an interpretative one: the lines are like those of rising smoke and thus indicate the purpose of the room. Another convincing element is the way in which the shelf units have been linked with the doorway arches. It is not clear whether the shelves are swelling powerfully against the wooden arches, or whether the arches press down to the extent that the shelves are forced to bend beneath them.

The designer confidently placed his motif on the wall between the two archways.

Sale-room for the Havana Company in Berlin, 1899

Reform dress, *c.* 1900

Part of Bruno and Paul Cassirer's reading-room in Berlin, 1898

Memorial plinth, Brussels, 1898

Candlestick, 1902

Lines of Force made Visible

It is impossible to ignore the structural drive in van de Velde's early work: it was a vigorous force which determined the form of most objects. Its direct expression was in lines, and the power with which the artist endowed each and every one of them. Van de Velde followed this doctrine rigidly, but with varying degrees of success. Sometimes the procedure made structural sense, but it could produce rhetorical, or merely illustrative forms. These levels of effect derived from one and the same intention, but were convincing to differing extents. They all appeared together on occasions when van de Velde failed to develop a room or object entirely from a single idea. The sum of the parts did not then produce a whole.

In the reading-room the tension within the door was extravagant but meaningful: it articulated the surface to the extent required by structural necessity. The questionable element is the overweighted proportions of the upper section. Similarly structurally supportive in conception were the three-dimensional forms on the edges of the panels and below the shelf above them. They

are statically of no consequence, but are visually striking, unveiling a flow of energy which seems immediately plausible. The eye and mind consent to follow these details and are grateful for their stimulating aid to understanding.

The candlestick can be seen as similarly heterogeneous. Even though it is unusual and surprising, the frame-like upper section is elegant, and also logically composed. Linear flow is held in permanent tension by alternately striving outwards and inwards. The upper bracket is important in this: it functions as the controlling force for the outward surge of movement below.

The tense form of the upper part hardly corresponds to the base, however. It developed three-dimensionally rather than structurally, probably with the intention of giving the necessary weight. It is obvious that its form was influenced by an earlier work by van de Velde, the memorial plinth for the heroic Belgian freedom fighter Mérode. The legitimately monumental quality of the plinth was bound to seem out of proportion if transferred to the base of a candlestick.

Candelabrum, 1902

Structural Skeletons

Van de Velde succeeded in translating linear structure into solid form in exemplary fashion with this sweeping candelabrum. A single movement, circling around itself, seems to seize the whole, and every detail is drawn into this flow. A powerful shaping force has also put its stamp on all the parts and left nothing unarticulated. In the upper section the movement swings out into space six times. The tense, structural organization is immediately evident; the object is almost exclusively a structural skeleton.

The hairdressing salon designed for Haby seizes space in the same way as the candelabrum. The lamps are the most clearly expressive feature, but the relief of other items also has the same effect. The wall of mirrors is graduated in so lively and striking a fashion that van de Velde was able to treat the tables used by the hairdressers as features within the scheme rather than having to pay attention solely to their function. All the services were run on the surface of the wooden wall of mirrors, and their elegant flow is clearly linked with the function of the taps and basins. The woodwork showed articulation typical of its designer, and now familiar.

Although the salon was only accessible to a very limited number of people, it was one of van de Velde's most popular works.

Haby's hairdressing salon in Berlin, 1901

Sculptural Form

The firm grasp of the three-dimensional which had become a characteristic of van de Velde's artistic hand increasingly affected his designs, and was applied to any material which can be shaped. This is true of both detail and the broader sweep. Thus the intricate modelling of the heater cover designed as a showcase in marble and bronze is the same as that found on earlier wooden fitments. Also, the somewhat slender excuse of needing an aperture, and a narrow one at that, to allow heat to escape has been used to justify an extravagantly sculptural design. The stone arch at the top, the distinct curve of the showcases, the massive quality of the bases and finally the way in which the heat outlet is constricted, all make a strong three-dimensional effect considerably enhanced by detail such as the lively pattern of the radiator grille, the columns inserted at the sides, the modelling of the stone and, last but not least, the curve of the mirror, double to contain the lower edge as well.

Smaller objects designed by van de Velde in the early years are also sculptural in form. Between 1899 and 1905 he produced numerous designs for ceramics, silver, porcelain and ivory, executed principally by firms in Thuringia. In almost every case the three-dimensional articulation of these objects has a functional justification. The cutlery is obviously intended to be comfortable and pleasing to hold, which is why the handle of the spoon is clearly different from those of the knife and fork. Van de Velde ignores the convention of making all the handles the same: he designs each item individually, then re-establishes the formal relationship by his treatment of line.

In the same way, similar but by no means identical ornamental forms connect the differently shaped items in the Meissen porcelain service. The circling motif on the plate corresponds with a staccato one on the containers. Derivation from the object's form is immediately recognizable in every case.

Three-dimensional design is particularly successful here and one special detail is extremely sensible: a tongue on the lid of the pot fits into the handle, and prevents the lid from moving around.

Showcase in the picture gallery of the Folkwang-Museum in Hagen, 1901

Items from a Meissen porcelain service, *c.* 1905

Items from a set of silver cutlery, 1903

Silver jardinière, part of a table set, 1902

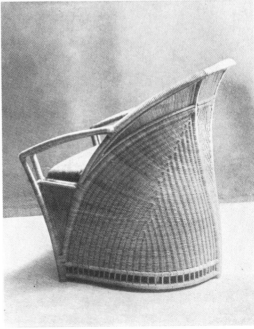

Two basketwork chairs,
c. 1905

Silver tea service with boxwood handles, 1905

Sliding Transitions

The supple, flowing plasticity of van de Velde's applied art increased, and is at its best completely free of superfluous matter. The silver jardinière is encircled by a line running around the entire oval of the vessel, allowing the handles to grow organically from the volume of the bowl. As is almost always the case with van de Velde, the decorative form works both as a sensuous enlivening device and as an indication of function.

The final absorption of ornament into form is demonstrated in the tea service. The gentle sweep of the objects seems to absorb anything not directly relevant. Only the handles are somewhat wilful, but even they are contained within the dominant outline. Co-ordination of contour and mass has succeeded admirably and the interplay of material and inspired form is evocative. One can imagine the objects in use; their outer flow symbolizes their purpose.

Henry van de Velde's three-dimensional ideas, for which metal was a particularly suitable medium, also found ready expression in the flexible cane used for basket-work.

Silver candelabrum, probably 1907

Over-interpretation

Van de Velde's liking for sweeping form did not altogether avoid the pitfall of designing shapes without content, which became an end in themselves, lacking the necessary functional motivation. The candelabrum carries an excess of metallic flesh, and one misses the firm structure of the earlier design on page 60 in particular. A shape suitable for plaster seems to have been imposed on silver in a way which does not make sense. Visual weight is greater than actual weight.

The museum hall was a daring attempt to transfer to architecture ideas developed for the smaller dimensions of applied art. The extravagant stucco is related to the base of the candelabrum and the articulation of the lamps is similar to the open structure of a belt buckle. However, what on an intimate scale was meaningful becomes rather heavy-handed and laboured on a larger one.

The polygonal ground plan is already familiar from Bloemenwerf. Van de Velde transformed the originally square room into a hexagon in order to conceal two less important doors by the insertion of piers (one of which can be seen on the upper left of the picture). However, the underlying aim was to make a space totally lacking in tension into a three-dimensional experience. He tried to justify the upwardly foaming scrolls by stating that they were intended to release the pictures from the walls and make it clear that these are not frescos, but paintings on canvas.

The museum hall was van de Velde's contribution to the great exhibition of applied art which took place in Dresden in 1906. The room only existed for the duration of the event. The nature of the occasion clearly seduced van de Velde into excesses of design. Otherwise, attempts to act in such a demonstrative manner were rare at this stage in his career.

Museum hall at the 'Kunstgewerbe' exhibition, Dresden, 1906

Machine room for the Harkort Company in Hagen, 1904

Rhythm and Tension

The dramatic features of the 1906 Dresden museum hall were intended by van de Velde as structural, and in this form were an extreme, representing the end of a line of development. The more austere, linear rather than three-dimensionally determined component in van de Velde's work had persisted despite this tendency. It had a clarity better suited to expressing structural ideas than were the denser sculptural condensations.

The articulation of the glass ceiling in the Harkort factory was obviously inspired by the tension of the drive belts. Here structurally necessary surface division seems to have been used as a stimulus to translate the rhythm of a machine room into a graphic picture.

The door furniture is another example of the way in which functional, structural and purely artistic ideas can complement and penetrate each other. The idea was probably to make the handles grow as logically as possible out of the surface, but also to emphasize them and make them noticed. This is also helped by the oval fields which give the complete design the necessary visual weight. We are thus dealing with function presented rhetorically, but ambivalent in origin. One element performs the function and another points it out. A precise contour firmly encloses the internal play of lines.

Door furniture for the Nietzsche archive in Weimar, 1903 ▷

Chair, 1898

Spatial Structures

The chair is a particularly good example of the translation of a concept which is linear and structural into articulated form: independently stable triangular links provide a lower section of great solidity. In a similar way the high back is supported by two vertical bars forming a spatial connection with it. A flow of forces can be seen quite clearly. In contrast with this it is logical that the seat has been inserted into the articulated system of the chair as a soft form without structural function. Only the two back supports rest upon it, and thus look springy and to a certain extent yielding.

The entire spatial structure is not spare, nor the most direct approach, as it were, but almost all the elements blend in gentle curves. This creates a structure entirely three-dimensional in conception. Only the horizontal bar between the legs seems somewhat hard and abrupt, but in contrast the movement from the back to the side supports of the seat is all the more supple. A necessary counterweight to the slender, upward-moving line is the protruding cross spar, which powerfully absorbs all vertical currents.

The details of the waiting-room are conceived in the same structural way as the chair. The sofa seems to be tethered in the corner, and the chair is a formally weaker variation of the other one.

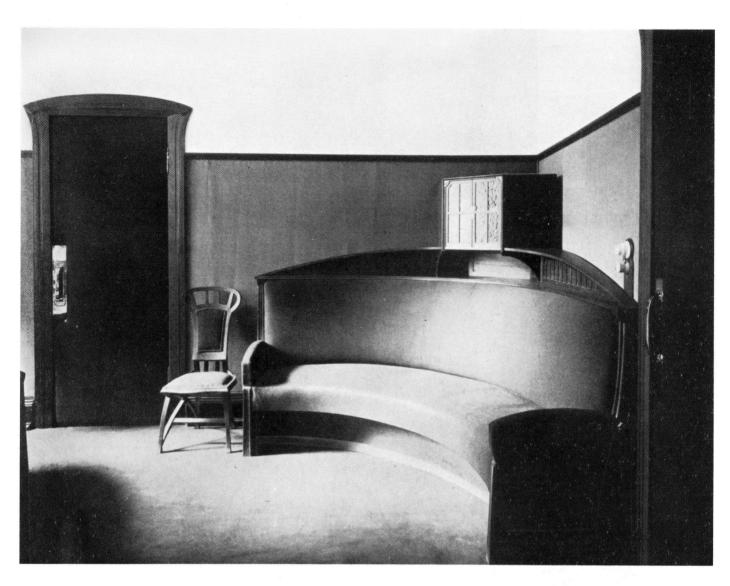

Corner sofa in the offices of Lübeck barrister Dr Wittern, 1902

Chair, 1898

71

Capital and staircase in the Folkwang-Museum in Hagen, 1901

Stair-well in the Folkwang-Museum in Hagen, 1901 ▷

The Folkwang-Museum as a Precedent

Henry van de Velde's most extensive opportunity to date to put his ideas into practice came from his patron Karl Ernst Osthaus' commission to design the interior of the new Folkwang-Museum. Three storeys of a building already complete as a shell were placed at his disposal. The various interior features – stucco cladding, banisters, balustrades and showcases – were designed individually and for an express purpose.

The detail of the wave movement rising with the steps of the staircase became very well known. The banister showed an exemplary application of the skeleton-like shaping of each element which was to become a hallmark of van de Velde.

Ceiling aperture and skylight in the Folkwang-Museum in Hagen, 1901

Silver belt buckle, before 1900

Upper hall of the Folkwang-Museum in Hagen, 1901

Spatial Interpenetration

The interlinked, three-dimensional structure of the banister rail is continued in the balustrade around the skylight providing light for the museum hall. Van de Velde had to take this on, along with other existing architectural features. It was not finally justified until the Belgian sculptor Georges Minne built a fountain underneath it (page 21).

The aperture itself stimulated van de Velde to a very inventive piece of design. The rail (now reconstructed) seems to be made up of a network in various layers, with individual strands running softly together. Inside the aperture the posts are continued downwards to form curved supports for the lamps which illuminate the fountain below. This created a more complex spatial relationship which is functionally as well as plastically unusual. It is reminiscent of the design of a piece of jewelry dating from before 1900. The complex line here is in fact continuous and uninterrupted. The invention of such a construction requires an unusually highly developed spatial imagination.

Music room in the Folkwang-Museum in Hagen, 1901

Fluent Connections

The rhetorical design of the museum interior came to rest in a windowless room at the back of the building apparently intended for small music groups. It was lit only from above, square in plan, and the cross-axes provided by the four doors made it very regular, a quality intensified by the identical design of the four corners. A rising and falling line ran around the room as a connecting feature, also passing through the door frames. Only the door jambs broke it up.

The handles on the main door of the museum show a related linear flow; their design shows how effortlessly van de Velde could adapt his line to very different purposes.

Handles on the main door of the Folkwang-Museum in Hagen, 1901

Design for a museum of applied art in Weimar, 1903/4

From Furniture to Architecture

Until 1903, van de Velde had worked in Germany only as a designer of interiors, furniture and applied art. He had, however, always intended to move into the sphere of architecture. The first designs for larger buildings, which appeared about this time, suggest that he saw his search for architectural form more as a change of course than needing a completely original approach. Van de Velde based his early buildings on furniture design, that is to say he used his experience in a sphere which he had already mastered. It is not only the details which are a reminder of his work in this area, but entire buildings, too.

The way in which the Kunstgewerbemuseum was to be articulated and its treatment of detail are also strikingly similar to van de Velde's ideas on interior design. The front of the building looks like a cabinet with glass inserts and the side wall like a showcase. Curves, also a van de Velde trade mark, appear in the design, but do not make much sense when translated into architecture. The windows, cut by a diagonal on either side of

the main door, would have been difficult to coordinate with the interior.

If one places the mirror showcase from the Folkwang-Museum (page 75) next to the side wall of the Weimar design, the relationship immediately becomes clear. Stabilizing elements are set in a relationship of tension with those which create movement. Between the massive piers of the façade, reminiscent of the open sections of the document cupboard illustrated, the walls seem like wooden panels, and the narrow gables at the ends of the front section are like the ends of a cupboard.

An earlier glazed cupboard can also be used as a comparison. Just as the supporting 'bridge' raises the piece of furniture off the floor, so a similar effect was probably intended in the architecture. The visual weight of the closed walls was in fact lightened by making them appear to flow towards the sides. The gentle upper section of the museum is also like the top of the cupboard.

Document cupboard, 1899

Cupboard, 1897

Garden side of Herbert Esche's house in Chemnitz, 1902/3

Counters in the Deutsche Bank in Augsburg, 1902

Ambivalent Transfer

The same observations as those made about the design of the Weimar Kunstgewerbemuseum are possible in the context of the first house which Henry van de Velde built in Germany. Here too, carpentry design was translated into stone. The gables are like cupboard fronts and the detailed, small-scale architecture of the bank counters could be a model intended for translation into a larger format. Uncertainty about scale seems to have dominated this process. If the crouching form of the Weimar museum was more like a piece of furniture than architecture, the villa on the other hand seems too spacious for its purpose, as though it was too large in all its dimensions.

Two details in particular suggest a comparison between architecture and furniture design: the lamp fixtures in the banking hall, and the garden fence of the villa are closely related in their basic structural idea. In each case an articulated structure is imposed upon a solid core, thus making the separation of differing formal and material functions very clear; this is a model which van de Velde subjected to continual variation.

Street side of Herbert Esche's house in Chemnitz, 1902/3

Wardrobe, 1903

In the music room of Herbert Esche's house in Chemnitz, 1902/3

Formal Paraphrases

Both interior and façade here are increasingly severe, reminiscent of a piece of apparatus or the bodywork of a car. The façade is almost a paraphrase of the fireplace surround, and the simple rhythms with which the windows are articulated seems to be borrowed from the bars on the rocking chair.

The architectural design was never realized, perhaps because it was thought to be too like a factory. It was a preliminary project for the Berlin Secession, in which Henry van de Velde – by his own admission – was involved with no great enthusiasm, because he thought that he would have no chance against two other competitors. Essentially, however, the design anticipates that of the Kunstschule in Weimar, built between 1904 and 1911 (page 111).

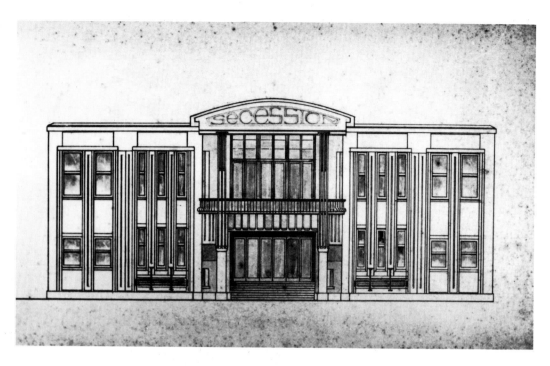

Design for a building for the Berlin Secession, 1904

Rocking chair, 1904

Boardroom for the Hagener Textilindustrie, 1905

From Rooms to Architecture

Van de Velde's characteristic ability to give his design a skeletal form, in which individual elements clearly demonstrate their various functions, is again shown here in a comparison of architecture and interior design. In the boardroom the ceiling light in particular takes full possession of the space which it occupies. The horizontal bars on the chairs can be interpreted in the same way. They not only strengthen the chair structurally, but make it appear lighter.

It is striking to see how these details are incorporated not only formally, but also structurally into the architecture. The early, faintly tent-like theatre design seems resolved, transparent and weightless, still free of all formative accretions. Comparing it with an apparently later version (page 89) we see the clear and unburdened early stages of an architectural idea.

The cross-section shows a highly three-dimensional approach, and the idea of the tripartite stage, later adopted, has already made an appearance.

Design for a theatre in Weimar, 1904

Incomplete cross-section of the Weimar theatre, 1904

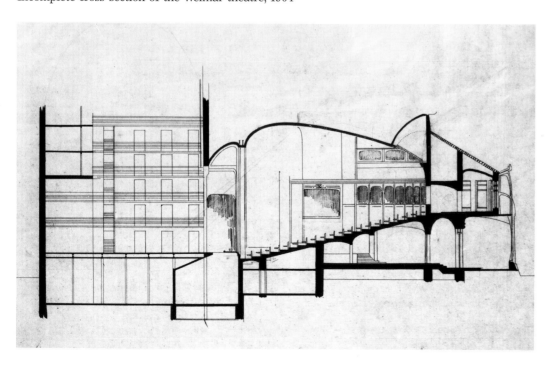

Chair and high desk, 1902/3

Changing Shapes

As van de Velde's experience increased, he drew his architectural form less and less from furniture design. Only the curve with the top sliced off in the middle section of the Leuring house is reminiscent of these origins. The striking feature now is an interplay of positive and negative spaces. Both the sofa and the central section of the house are flanked by relatively severe elements, between which the centre seems all the more animated. Though formally similar, the two volumes have been set in opposition to each other.

In contrast with van de Velde's previous procedure, the writing desk can be seen as the transfer of architectural discipline to a piece of furniture. The apparently simple design in fact contains a high degree of formal differentiation – in the articulation of the side sections, for example, and the resolution of the base. A vital factor is the angled design, which seems to enclose the user. This piece of furniture was used by both van de Velde and Graf Kessler in their studies.

Street side of the Leuring house in Scheveningen, 1902

Sofa with side sections, shortly after 1900 (see also page 46)

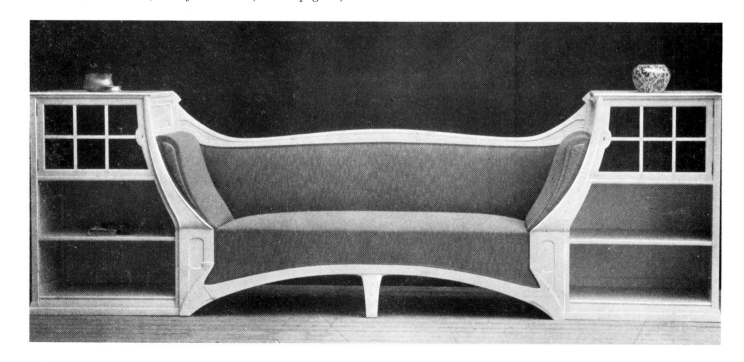

Room in the Nietzsche archive in Weimar, 1903

Successful Translation

Henry van de Velde found the way to architectural form when he succeeded in translating to buildings not only the detail of the structural discipline of his rooms, but the entire principle. This sometimes came about – as in the example of this theatre design – as the result of a logical reversal of interior and exterior. All the elements which in the room in the Nietzsche archive were used to articulate, bear and scan, appear in the theatre design with similar function, but as it were in inverted form. And the correspondence goes further. The sweep of the sofa is repeated in the bulge of the façade, the cavetto moulding in the room corresponds to the rounded upper part of the façade. In the room the 'open' corners are filled with articulating elements; in the building they are opened right out, in accordance with their quite different intention.

The theatre design is equal in boldness to the structural elegance of the room. These two designs were high points in van de Velde's work, which had here at last escaped from the realm of the dilettante.

Design for a theatre in Weimar, 1904

Henry van de Velde with a group of people who were particulary close to him in Weimar: seated extreme left Harry Graf Kessler, standing the painter Ludwig von Hofmann, seated right the stage reformer Edward Gordon Craig; centre a model for the theatre in Weimar (see also page 85); probably 1904

Work for Friends

Henry van de Velde enjoyed considerable esteem in Berlin in 1900/1, but this could be regarded as a misunderstanding. Properly speaking, what he had achieved here was a hollow success: he had set off on his travels in order to win large numbers of people over to his ideas of artistic reform, but had acquired only a very small clientele. Van de Velde, still full of praise for William Morris, found himself in a position similar to that which the Englishman had experienced not long before. He was supported by an élite, but not by society as a whole.

Undoubtedly the circles who encouraged van de Velde in Berlin were particularly susceptible to his ideas, though for differing reasons. There was a mixture of commercial and social, and some artistic, interests. The Keller & Reiner gallery, the court hairdresser François Haby and the Havana Company probably commissioned him to design their premises to be *en vogue*, rather than for any other reason. They were concerned to attract attention. When van de Velde came up with particularly imaginative designs for these commissions his clients' speculative expectations were certainly fulfilled. He was to some extent striving for effect, however, and thus confirmed some of the louder *nouveau-riche* traits of which Berlin was rather fond at the time. In fact there was a community of interest, as the still-youthful metropolis was generous enough to celebrate van de Velde's experiments as well as to support them. In contrast with Paris, Berlin made the artist feel recognized.

Interior designs executed by van de Velde for private individuals in this period turned out to be less spectacular. They show the designer's lack of proper involvement. The results seem laboured, somehow incomplete. A possible exception is Harry Graf Kessler's residence in the Köthener Strasse; a surviving photograph shows that it may well have been elegant, light and witty. It is clear that here van de Velde had found a client who responded to him with sensitivity and paid him proper attention. The two men became friends.

Kessler and van de Velde resembled each other physically, and must have been similar types, united by related aims. They apparently shared the idea that the metropolis should be a stimulating and socially active place, but contradictorily, essentially schizophrenically, were both happy to escape from it and find solitude in which to devote themselves to concentrated work. They had grown closer in Berlin, but soon left the city to move to Weimar. Perhaps, as outsiders, there was also an unspoken desire to be at the centre of events, but at the same time to find in a life of withdrawal the protection which they lacked because of their unstable existence. Both men were immigrants: Kessler, though German by origin, was brought up in England and had developed in very cosmopolitan fashion. Wilhelmine Berlin must have seemed both rich and cheap to him; he obviously remained a stranger there. He did not spend any length of time in the city until later, after 1920. Like him, van de Velde was an artist focused upon England, similarly looking for a home other than his natural one. Both were

Work in Weimar began in 1902, and continued until 1917. Commissions there included furnishings for Harry Graf Kessler's flat (1902) and in 1903 the Nietzsche archive for Elisabeth Förster-Nietzsche, the poet-philosopher's sister; 1903/4 saw designs for a summer theatre, a new arts and crafts museum and a tourist restaurant (none built). In 1903 van de Velde journeyed to the East on the invitation of Albert Ballin, director of the Hamburg-America Line; he was involved in the foundation of the Deutscher Kulturbund in Weimar, which took place under the influence of Harry Graf Kessler. In 1902 he built houses for J. W. Leuring in Scheveningen and Herbert Esche in Chemnitz.

'During one of my stays in Paris around that time I received the following letter from Harry Kessler, written in Weimar on 6 December 1905: "While you, my dear friend, are drifting around elegant Parisian venues, the most amazing things are happening here…! Madame van de Velde probably told you that Max Reinhardt is in Weimar. Yesterday Hofmannsthal and I showed him your theatre models. He was completely won over. He thinks that your approach is elegant and simple, and perceived the 'dramatic' beauty of the architectural form. The Nietzsche archive whipped his enthusiasm to new heights. This morning I took him to the Wickel and suggested to him without any more ado that he should commission you to rebuild the Emberg hall by the Deutsches Theater, which he has acquired. He wants to turn it into a small theatre seating about four hundred people. Understandably his reply was that he couldn't commit himself before he'd seen you and found out whether you'd be interested in the job, and he would like you to visit him in Berlin as soon as you get back from Paris."'
Memoirs, page 268 ff.

Harry Graf Kessler, painted by Edvard Munch, 1904

'The relationship between Graf Kessler and myself was in the first place reticent and cautious. The first impression was one of profound distance, impossible to bridge. Although we felt ourselves bound by close ties in an almost fraternal, unassailable friendship, this feeling of distance persisted throughout almost forty years of close association. Physically Kessler had perfect poise and natural, understated elegance. He was probably a little smaller than the average, but well proportioned with no trace of corpulence. Penetrating, gleaming eyes without a shade of hardness looked out of a handsome face; sometimes an authoritarian trait could be detected. If one were to look for similar figures in literature, one would turn to Oscar Wilde's "Dorian Gray" or Joris K. Huysmans' "Des Esseintes", the principal character in his novel *A Rebours*.'
Memoirs, page 159 ff.

Harry Graf Kessler was born on 23 May 1868 in Paris; his father was German, his mother Irish; first critical essays on art in the periodical *Pan* from 1895; co-operated with Hugo von Hofmannsthal on libretti for *Josephslegende* and *Rosenkavalier*; founded the Cranach Press in Weimar; from 1918 to 1921 ambassador to Poland, supported the concept of the League of Nations, later emigrated to Majorca, died on 30 November 1937 in Lyon. Author of *Notizen über Mexico* (1898); *Walther Rathenau* (1928); *Gesichter und Zeiten, Erinnerungen* (1935); *Tagebücher 1918–1937* appeared in 1961.

fated to be wanderers throughout their lives – Kessler the diplomat, patron and vulnerable aesthete, who lived in Berlin, Paris and Warsaw and finally went into exile on Majorca; van de Velde, the man of letters, artist-designer and aesthete too, who worked in Belgium, Germany, France, Holland and then back in Belgium again.

The two men also shared a longing for France. Kessler was a lover of Impressionist painting, and tried to make converts in Berlin; van de Velde had found some of his most important stimuli in Paris, and the lively colour of his interiors was a result of his artistic experiences there. The lifestyle of both men drew them westwards, and yet their insights and reason bound them to Central Europe. Germany offered them a real base for their intermediary activities, and this was clearly more important to them than the brilliance of a city which already had more than its share of artists. What was there in Paris that they could change? What made them any different in that city from countless similar, indeed kindred spirits?

As well as all this, the two men had a common taste for proselytizing. Kessler was in addition a keen patron and stimulator of others, but kept to the background himself – except as a writer; van de Velde on the other hand saw the development of doctrine as his vocation. One of his most beautiful statements of faith – the text called *Amo* – was printed in 1909 by the Cranach Press in Weimar, founded by Kessler. Bibliophile printing was apparently the only passion which this man, who looks so restrained in his pictures, displayed openly.

Harry Graf Kessler's homosexuality was probably another important factor for a man inclined to choices which were at once sensitive and determined. His relationship with van de Velde was a means of sublimation which translated the erotic into the spiritual aesthetic. As direct fulfilment was out of the question, such transposition could be pursued all the more resolutely, with private matters kept unequivocally in the background. At the same time, however, a closeness based on related aspirations was at the root of everything which united the two men. This special association also had the advantage of freedom from financial obligation. Kessler's fortune was limited in scope: he was more a catalyst than a man who could realize great projects. However, the idea of building a Nietzsche stadium in Weimar gave rather more extravagant form to his expectations. The notion originated in his pedagogic eroticism: the idea was to build a new Hellas. Temple, arena and stand were to be united in a building intended to serve both sport and spiritual education. The ideal behind the plan was a symbiosis of physical and spiritual discipline.

It could have been no ordinary task to design domestic interiors for a man with ideas of this kind, and one which could only be realized on the basis of subtle observation, an ability to perceive the occupant's requirements and fears simultaneously. An opportunity arose for the first time in Berlin – although, as already stated, we know little of the outcome – and a second time in Weimar, after Kessler had accepted the invitation to become director of the Kunstgewerbemuseum there in 1901.

He had already intervened on van de Velde's behalf with the Grand Duke before this. The artist was commissioned to build a college for the applied arts, a training-ground for the taste of local craftsmen – with the intention of making them competitive again. He was also promised various architectural projects. Thus van de Velde must have felt himself closer to his original intentions in Weimar than in Berlin; he had an opportunity of working on a broader scale. His time in Weimar began full of hope. Expectations were further raised by the traditions of the place: a new artistic heyday would have chimed perfectly with the image of the town. It should also not be forgotten that the end-of-an-era solidity which informed the little court at the time affected van de Velde very deeply. The loving zeal with which he describes these years in his memoirs can be read and understood in no other way. Apparently his stay there brought him happiness in the early days; Kessler's view was more sober, directed rather to how the town could be of use to him.

When Kessler asked van de Velde to design the interior of his house in Weimar too the two men already knew each other well enough for neither to need converting to the other's ideas. The result was correspondingly relaxed and natural, and the house makes an impression of refreshing effortlessness. We sense that for the first time van de Velde felt bound by no particular expectations, and therefore did not need to prove anything. Overall design and details cohere in a surprisingly simple way. The reticence of the design perhaps makes the house less 'revolutionary' than previous work, but on closer inspection we can see that its novel quality lies in brilliant simplicity, and no longer in striving after effect.

So were things now on a different footing? It would be easy to conclude that once van de Velde felt he was receiving due recognition and was working in a friendly atmosphere he was able to shed many of his earlier idiosyncrasies. Did the artist, now part of a community which understood him, feel that he was delivered from a number of things – including himself? Under close consideration, however, this new way of working was a step backwards, potentially important and helpful as an interim experience, but only on the understanding that it was not in itself the goal. If the rooms designed for Graf Kessler are a far cry from the gentle, intellectual classicism we find in Alfred Walther Heymel's house, which made similar demands, the design does tend to suggest a model which could be seen as excessively private. Consequently the question arises of whether the intensive calm which van de Velde was aiming for in association with his friend Kessler was suited to work on a larger scale.

First attempts to design buildings to surpass the Bloemenwerf house got off to a shaky start. The house built by van de Velde in 1903 for the Chemnitz textile manufacturer Herbert Esche is generously proportioned, practical and exceedingly functional, but both ground plan and façade look as though they have been assembled from a kit, and lack a sense of unity (which meant that the house did not have to be completed immediately; it was possible to extend it many years later). The extent to which ideas derived from furniture manufacture were involved in its design can also be clearly seen.

It also shows, however, that the client's confidence in his architect gave the latter courage to break through previous boundaries. The house gives the impression of being bold, spacious and confident; everyone who was involved took risks and aimed for a surprisingly unconventional end product. However, it did not seem to inspire imitation; it must quickly have emerged that the various aspects developed in isolation could not necessarily be transferred to other projects.

Most of the drawings for the summer theatre which the actress Louise Dumont intended to build in Weimar, in order to hold a festival similar to Bayreuth there, seem to be feeling their way to a large extent. They can be seen only as an approximation, but despite the tentative nature of the ground plan there are two surprisingly confident suggestions for façades. This gives the impression that there was an overall vision, but lack of professionalism prevented delivery of the details. Van de Velde was later to show an ability to handle these as well. The development process was surely supported by artists encouraged to visit Weimar by Kessler – Edward Gordon Craig stayed there in 1904, for example. They gave van de Velde advice and courage.

Seen in this light, the early days in Weimar were hopeful ones. In addition they confirmed van de Velde's ability to build the Kunstgewerbeschule and the first phase of the Kunstschule. Up to this point Kessler's advice to choose Weimar as his place of work had certainly been good. But by giving this advice Kessler had also acquired permanent responsibility for the artist.

The resulting close relationship between the two men underwent a conspicuous setback after a few years, however: the situation at court – the plane on

In Harry Graf Kessler's Berlin flat, before 1900; on the left is the partially unrolled picture *The Models* by Georges Seurat

Nietzsche stadium, pages 162–63
Esche house, pages 80–82
Weimar theatre, pages 85 and 89
Art school buildings in Weimar, pages 109–12

Rudolph Alexander Schröder, Heymel residence in Munich, 1901

which they both existed – altered fundamentally. The early death of the Grand Duchess – in 1905, after a short marriage – removed the cultivated influence which she had exerted over her husband, who tended to indifference in artistic matters. The climate of the court changed radically, and further thoughts of a 'New Weimar' were pushed into the background for the time being. Dislike of the arts eventually assumed quite ridiculous proportions, and led to an incident in 1907 which appeared to have been planned down to the last detail. While the Grand Duke was away hunting in India, Harry Graf Kessler persuaded the sculptor Auguste Rodin to dedicate a nude drawing to the Duke – on the touching assumption that the latter would be impressed by it on his return. The opposite turned out to be the case. Kessler fell from favour and lost all his influence at court. A high official who had played the intriguer in the Grand Duke's absence died before Kessler could issue a heroic challenge to a duel. The Weimar drama had became a farce, and each new scene became harder for van de Velde to play. Kessler continued to live in Weimar, but that was little help. The basis of their friendship had not disappeared, but its special motivation had: they could hardly hope to achieve anything further as a team. Kessler's wild plan to build a stadium in Weimar in honour of Friedrich Nietzsche with van de Velde's help therefore seems a desperate attempt to bring about the impossible. The idea dates from 1911, four years after the Rodin affair, but it was never realized.

A double page from *Amo*, text and design by Henry van de Velde, printed in an edition of 150 copies at Harry Graf Kessler's Cranach Press in Weimar in 1909

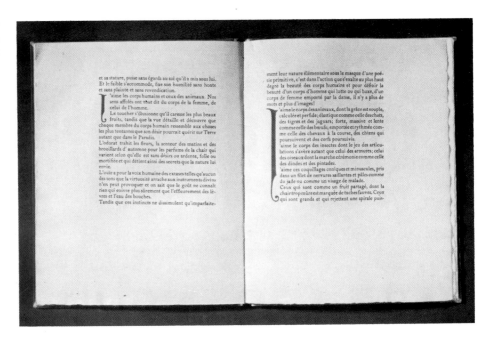

94

In Graf Kessler's flat in Weimar, 1902

Living-room in Graf Kessler's flat in Weimar

Graf Kessler's Flat in Weimar, 1902

Here – as was the case with most early commissions – the design had to be adapted to the original building. However, it would seem that Henry van de Velde made only minor alterations to the flat in Cranachstrasse which Harry Graf Kessler had rented.

The modest proportions of the rooms permitted pleasingly effortless décor. A small number of well-designed pieces of furniture were arranged as their function suggested. A 'spatial law' could only be seen in the restrained sub-division of the walls. Ornamental orchestration was not attempted. It is clear that this flat is intended for somebody whose confidence van de Velde had long enjoyed and that in working for him the effort to win someone over was completely absent.

It appears that shortly after completion of the first phase, Kessler increased the number of rooms which van de Velde was to design for him. In the course of this, the dining-room became a living-room, but Maurice Denis's picture stayed where it was. Its arcadian mood was perfectly complemented by Aristide Maillol's figure of a youth; the plaster detail from the Parthenon frieze above the fireplace to an extent confirmed that this was a modern version of a 'Greek' room. These three works of art set the room on a fairly high plane, but did not dominate it. Its flexibility as a space for relaxed living was brought about above all by the arrangement of the furniture, which did not have to be in fixed positions. Individual small lamps were spread around the room.

Other details contributed to this relaxed quality: the simple contours of the wooden panelling, taken up in the pedestal; the fireplace surround, almost English in its plainness; and the simple framing for the window. It was very advanced to cover the floors of this room, and indeed all the other rooms in the flat, with matting running through the doorways without a seam.

◁ The same part of the room that appears on page 95, now a living-room

Study

Graf Kessler's Flat in Weimar, 1902

The picture shows the study years after its completion. It seems that from the outset the room was intended to be used for work rather than to impress. The desk was designed as unit furniture, and a visual finish to the open end is achieved with a few struts, responding to each other in severe rhythm. The chair design is from the Munich study of 1899 (page 53). By the window is a version of the desk used by van de Velde himself (page 86). The bookcase has been extended; it ended originally with the cupboard section.

The rather conventional seating arrangement in the anteroom does not seem as strange as the artistic demands of the period might have suggested, because it forms the centre of an interior design not aimed at avant-garde declamation,

but more concerned with logically subtle detail. Van de Velde never hesitated to appropriate forms proven in use and meaning, but always tried to adapt them to his characteristically three-dimensional sensibilities. The particular effect of the group of seats is based on the tension between the different curves.

The basketwork furniture in the background, designed by van de Velde for mass production by Bosse of Weimar (page 64), is more individual in concept. The pliable material was better suited to his ideas for the use of space than relatively rigid wood, which can only be given plasticity by working it down from a larger volume.

The dining-room furniture in its new arrangement can be seen through the open door.

Anteroom

In the library

Graf Kessler's Flat in Weimar, 1902

The library was a small room, and therefore almost all the furniture was built in. It is thus clear why the picture over the sofa was subordinated to the wall by its mounting. If it had been hung normally it would probably have been excessively conspicuous. Typical of van de Velde's functional procedure was the setting of graphics in the panels of the sliding doors. This notion is reminiscent of similar design in the boardroom of the Cassirer publishing house (page 58).

The emphatically concave sofa looks inviting: one senses a challenge to sit down and spread out one's arms. The rounded back creates two spandrels, on one of which a small sculpted head is placed; Kessler could admire it in profile when sitting sideways on the sofa.

The picture on the right shows the dining-room furniture illustrated on page 95 in a new arrangement, more severe in its structural articulation than in the room it occupied previously. It is anything but rigid, however. The wall covering is

clearly put together from units, and looks as though it is removable. This impression and the logically simple form give the room a Japanese look, enhanced by the sideboard and mats. The fact that picture hooks can be hung on the shallow strips of the wall cladding contributes to the emphatically functional organization of the room.

A similar point can be made about the chairs as about the seating in the anteroom. The chairs' Chippendale-like form seemed to van de Velde to need modification, but not to be changed completely. The division of the back is particularly successful.

The gracious, clearly articulated sideboard, tending to the Japanese in style, is one of the earliest pieces of furniture designed by van de Velde. A similar piece, narrower and with slightly different details, was a feature of the flat which he designed for Kessler in Berlin.

Dining-room ▷

100

Henry van de Velde in his studio on the upper
floor of the Kunstgewerbeschule in Weimar,
probably 1907. He is surrounded by his own
pictures and photographs of his work (Esche
house in Chemnitz, sale-room for the Havana
Company in Berlin); on the left is a model of a
theatre auditorium; on the desk in the foreground are designs for the de luxe edition of
Friedrich Nietzsche's *Also sprach Zarathustra*
(Leipzig, 1908); on the drawing-board leaning
against the desk probably a drawing for alterations to the Landesmuseum in Weimar (1907/8)

Structural Elegance and Material Economy

At the beginning of the Weimar period Henry van de Velde was in a position to prove for the first time that he was not just a versatile interior designer, but also an architect. Until then he had built only the Villa Bloemenwerf (or co-operated on other commissions), which could be considered an achievement which demonstrated his enthusiasm but was rather a fluke. All that it proved was that it was the work of a gifted dilettante.

It is clear – as already mentioned – from the first buildings built or designed by van de Velde in Germany, that they were based on ideas drawn from his furniture. This is particularly clear in the case of Herbert Esche's house in Chemnitz, built in 1902/3, and the 1903/4 Kunstgewerbemuseum in Weimar, and it might have been suspected that he would never be able to design independently conceived buildings. He dispelled these doubts with two buildings which demanded functional planning, rather than individual and artistic design. The challenge lay in the fact that they were on a larger scale than anything he had previously designed, and had to be more neutral because of their function. Despite this both the Kunstschule in Weimar and the Chemnitz tennis clubhouse could have been considerably more lavish. Their relative restraint is certainly not based on external constraints, but is a conscious decision on the part of their designer. Clearly he felt their design to be a response to the purposes which they had to serve. There is no sense of artistic sacrifice – on the contrary, it seems that van de Velde had for the first time found work in which his intentions could be more clearly expressed than had been the case with previous commissions. The leap into public activity, as opposed to just generally being known, could now be made.

The two buildings mentioned above show an emphatically structural tendency, and thus involved van de Velde in contemporary artistic discussion. They brought him close to Peter Behrens and Otto Wagner, established, trend-setting architects. The Chemnitz tennis club has a marked affinity with the Modern Viennese movement, and may indeed have been ahead of it. The precision of the work, both inside and out, makes it similar to the 'engineering' style of the buildings for which Otto Wagner was responsible at that time (stations on the Viennese S-Bahn and the weir on the Danube canal). This is true of the cubic, yet richly articulated, design, the striking use of iron, and also of details such as the lamps on the terrace and the geometrical design on the windowless wall, of a formal severity surprisingly unusual in van de Velde's work, and suggesting a conscious quotation – or tribute.

A comparison between the dining-room in Esche's house in Lauterbach and Otto Wagner's Vienna Postsparkasse shows a similar approach. Both give an impression of predominantly technical detail, as though they could be unscrewed and individual parts interchanged. The wall slabs, canopies and cornices of Otto Wagner's building correspond to van de Velde's interior decoration. There is no longer a particular distinction between interior and exterior; architectural principles are applied to décor and vice versa.

In 1904 building started on the Kunstschule in Weimar (completed 1911), and also work on the interior of the Schede house in Wetter on the Ruhr. In 1905/6 the Kunstgewerbeschule in Weimar was built. In 1906 van de Velde was involved in the 'Deutsche Kunstgewerbe' exhibition in Dresden: museum hall, two interiors, individual pieces of furniture. From 1906 to 1908 he built the Chemnitz tennis club, 1906 an interior for Curt von Mutzenbecher in Wiesbaden, and in 1907/8 worked on an interior for Arnold Esche's country house in Lauterbach/Thuringia and designs for rebuilding the Landesmuseum in Weimar (not realized). In 1907 he was appointed representative of the Deutscher Werkbund in Thuringia.

Esche house, pages 80–82
Museum in Weimar, page 78
Tennis club, pages 113–19

Otto Wagner, hot-air blower in the Postsparkasse in Vienna, 1904–6

Dining-room in Arnold Esche's house in Lauterbach/Thuringia, 1907/8

'I tell you that the time will come when the furnishing of a prison cell by Professor Van de Velde will be considered an aggravation of the sentence.'
Adolf Loos, quoted from Kenneth Frampton, *Modern Architecture*, London, 1978

Adolf Loos was an extremely controversial figure, both as an architect and as author of critical essays on cultural matters. He was born in Brünn in 1870, studied for a brief period in Dresden and went to the USA in 1893, where he was to spend three adventurous years. His confrontation with architecture at the Chicago School influenced his entire future development. From 1896 onwards he worked in Vienna, where he opposed the Secession (Hoffmann, Olbrich). His creed was probably most clearly formulated in the essay 'Ornament und Verbrechen' (1908). The relatively few buildings he designed had a characteristic cubic shape and were unusually austere. He also liked to use classical elements almost as quotations (which led to a strange design for a high-rise building in the form of a Doric column). From 1923 he lived in Paris in contact with representatives of Esprit Nouveau and the Dadaists, but had no success. Some of his best buildings date from after his return. His later years were overshadowed by a private scandal. He died in Vienna, a city he had probably always hated, in 1933.

The interior of the tennis club and the rooms in Esche's house would also have appealed to another Viennese architect, Adolf Loos (had he been prepared to take notice of them!). His famous and foolish remark about the particular applications of van de Velde's ornamentation doubtless referred to earlier work. As frequently occurs – and particularly in Loos's case – the violence of the response shows more what the two men had in common than what divided them. For Adolf Loos, any person who was akin to him by virtue of being an artist, but who did not follow exactly the same line in his work, was a greater enemy than any other; he saw such a person as an apostate, and that was worse than lack of talent. His invective is reserved for artists of his own calibre.

Both artists were self-taught and had derived considerable experience from a kind of voluntary exile – Loos had spent three years in the USA and van de Velde had been in rural retreat at the same time. This had given Loos a pragmatic, emphatically functional turn of mind (which did not exclude conservative elements) and made van de Velde an artistic missionary who claimed to act with great rationality. Loos was less prophetic, but had a highly polemical streak, and thus found more sympathy at first; he was more direct, and did not use the ornate circumlocutions which van de Velde still found necessary. What they had in common was the twin gift of being able to put things into practice as well as to persuade. The consequence of this, however, was a conflict between the notion as put into words and its realization. Both artists were criticized because of this. They could, it is true, always claim that they had been imperfectly understood, but both invoked to the same extent the danger of excessive personal precommitment. Only those close to them knew that their ostensible vanity concealed great insecurity. Both men were far too clever and too free from the conventional naïveté of the artist not to be able to sense the shakiness of the ground upon which they trod. Thus they were continually being forced to defend themselves, even after apparent victories. It should again be emphasized that this constant state of irritation was bound to drive them apart rather than bring them together, as neither could be a support for the other.

The work executed by the two artists was also related in some ways. They had come to architecture via interior decoration, and the disciplines easily overlapped with each other, although not always in an appropriate fashion. Loos was not afraid to use stone as if it were wood and wood as if it were stone – he stuck heavy marble under ceilings and used wooden elements of such solidity, density and size that they looked as though they were made of stone. Van de Velde, on the other hand, designed entire houses as though they were pieces of furniture, and later allowed his architectural experience to influence his interior design. He liked using wood as though it were iron and stone as a material which could happily take on any form – against its nature. There is no doubt that this process was enriching and stimulating, but for a long time a lack of professionalism was apparent, and was responsible for several mistakes alongside the successes.

For van de Velde there is a tension, resolved only in his best work, between essential modesty of purpose and extravagant design, and there is a similar, though inverse, tension in the work of Loos. In the latter case simple forms were called upon to accommodate an interior life which was much too complicated for them. The discrepancy between the determined plainness of his exteriors and the imaginative 'spatial plan' of the interior cannot be ignored – not only the 'floating' arrangement of the windows, but also more generally in the tricks used to imply unity where essentially there is diversity. Van de Velde, on the other hand, liked to create contradictions where a solution was already present in essence; this is disquietingly borne out by the emphatic quality of his monumental planning.

In a period in which they were both almost forgotten – the early 1920s – each of the architects suffered a major setback: Loos designed the *Chicago Tribune* building, van de Velde planned the Kröller-Müller museum. Both were outdated concepts, though in veiled form, and in the case of Loos a form which was witty and consequently almost acceptable. But they were also monuments to the desperation caused by the fall from grace of two ageing artists. It is almost as though this bitterness were necessary, however, so that they could later rise from the ashes purified: the biographies of both Loos and van de Velde show that both men made a surprising comeback in the late 1920s. Some of their best buildings date from this period, late for both of them.

Both artists had achieved a surprising amount with relatively few buildings. Their famous colleagues in Berlin and Vienna had been much more successful in terms of number of commissions, but had seldom aroused the same degree of interest as did the house in the Vienna Michaelerplatz, for example, or the Werkbund theatre in Cologne. In both cases the challenge had been considerable, regardless of the extent to which the buildings were successful in detail. They were not just simply buildings, but multiform artistic manifestations in the sense that

Adolf Loos, Kärntner Bar in Vienna, 1907

Hoenderloo museum, pages 172–77

Living-room in Arnold Esche's house in Lauterbach/Thuringia, 1907/8

Garden side of the Schinckel house in Hamburg, 1926

Dressing table at the Hohenhof, Hagen, 1907/8

they incorporated their surroundings, history and related disciplines – the kind of work which, it would seem, can only be realized by educated and tested dilettantes, that is to say, designers who are able to ignore specialist problems to an appropriate extent. In each case it was not the degree of perfection which was important but the enormous impetus each building had, liberation through confusion.

Adolf Loos and Henry van de Velde also shared a deep-rooted homelessness. It is true that Loos came back from America to Austria, and then lived successfully in Vienna, which was particularly suited to his literary temperament, but he remained alien as an architect. He may have felt better understood after 1923 in Paris, but he was in fact to receive his most important commissions from the territory of the former Austro-Hungarian Empire. The Belgian van de Velde had chosen Germany as the most suitable place for his work, but presumably more from insight than from inclination – which in his case too was towards France. Belgium was eventually to restore the balance; he returned there late, and after a detour via Holland. In both cases there had been long periods of wandering which were unusual to this extent for artists.

Through personal inclination, but also as a result of their itinerant lifestyle, both Loos and van de Velde had connections with the most varied artistic circles. They were as familiar with European drama, literature and fine art as with architecture and with luxury and traditional crafts. They were equally able to formulate judgments about morals and fashion as they were to pronounce on the character and abilities of individuals. Loos was a close friend of Karl Kraus, and a committed observer of the entire Viennese cultural scene; in Paris he had designed houses for Tristan Tzara and Josephine Baker, and the leading lights of the Esprit Nouveau and members of the Surrealist movement were part of his circle. Van de Velde knew Hugo von Hofmannsthal and met him regularly, and Louise Dumont and Edward Gordon Craig had visited him in Weimar. Through Harry Graf Kessler he had made the acquaintance of numerous French artists, especially Aristide Maillol. In such cases it made no difference whether they met in Weimar or Paris. In the early planning stages for the Théâtre des Champs-Elysées, van de Velde had met Maurice Denis and even, through Victor and Natasha de Golubeff, Gabriele d'Annunzio (although in the latter case with mixed feelings). It matters little whether or not these and many other encounters led to permanent relationships; they created circles and established connections of a truly international nature.

As both men were aware of being known artists, but were insecure and to some extent not properly established, they had an understandable desire to gather pupils around them. Loos did this within a private foundation, and van de Velde rather more officially, under the auspices of the Weimar Kunstgewerbeschule. As almost always happens, this attempt to achieve continuity of one's own thought by personal contact also failed in the present cases. Neither Loos nor van de Velde lived on to any marked extent in their pupils; they were presumably too complicated as teachers and confusing as models. Though they may have had principles at their disposal, they did not have the consistency which younger people felt they should be able to expect.

The small scale of the Kunstgewerbeschule shows how limited was van de Velde's following in Weimar. Its only decoration, the unifying, circular motif of the arch, is thus almost symbolic. If this building is like a workshop, the Kunstschule opposite is almost like a factory. This impression is caused above all by the large, very simply divided windows. The effect is moderated, though only to a certain extent, by the plasticity of some sections, which have greater volume than that required by statics. This gives the architecture expressive traits which are strikingly inartistic in execution. The suppressed drama of the Weimar Kunstschule is faintly reminiscent of the AEG turbine room in Berlin, built by Peter Behrens in the same period. In both these cases, technical form is sustained

visually by flanking, bastion-like additions, which at the same time increase its expressiveness. The self-restraint which van de Velde achieved despite everything is most clearly recognizable in the 'unresolved' treatment of the piers, which especially in the central section look as though they have been truncated and not completed. In fact there was nothing to necessitate greater extravagance of design.

The extent to which architectural discipline was taken can be seen in a comparison with the Glasgow School of Art, built from 1898 to 1908 by Charles Rennie Mackintosh and certainly known to van de Velde when he completed his design in 1910, which he could have changed as a result. Weimar's reply to the richly faceted play of the Scottish building is a design strikingly similar in dimensions, but artistically antithetical. Van de Velde approached the commission in quieter fashion and created a working building. Mackintosh, on the other hand, used the occasion for an artistic demonstration: art can only be created inside emphatically artistic architecture. He successfully anticipated what others had still to create.

This is the period of the foundation of the Deutscher Werkbund (1907 in Munich). Van de Velde was not a founder member, but it must have greatly appealed to him. He was soon very active within it. Both the ethical goals of the association – the encouragement of good design without an outdated renunciation of the machine – and also its social basis – which involved interested parties from all circles, and not just artists – corresponded almost exactly with his own notions. The association's club-like character permitted a concentrated exchange of views, and the current arguments confirmed many of his own ideas. The artist, who had hitherto been somewhat isolated, consequently found himself accepted by a society in which he could provide universal artistic stimulus.

His commitment reached a peak in the famous Cologne Werkbund dispute of 1914. It seemed that the eloquent agitator who spoke out against Hermann Muthesius's proposals for stylization was no longer the rational figure of the period from 1904 to 1910. This impression could stem from the fact that the two opponents took up positions which decidedly did not represent their real opinions. Setting ideas against each other which were by no means mutually exclusive, they caused a conflict which in essence became a comparison of competing artists. Van de Velde justifiably felt superior to Muthesius as an architect, and Muthesius for his part presumably had little sympathy for the particular

Kunstschule in Weimar, 1904–11; figure in the foreground by sculptor Richard Engelmann

Charles Rennie Mackintosh, Glasgow Art School, 1898–1908

Werkbund principles, page 189

Peter Behrens, AEG turbine room in Berlin, 1909

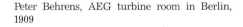

characteristics of the Belgian, who in his view had long ago betrayed their common model, England. But what Muthesius took very literally – as his Berlin country houses show – van de Velde had translated into a general maxim for designers. The very functional works he produced between 1904 and 1910 could not serve as patterns for stylization, but had at the same time the character of models, and were formally independent. They were examples of extremely rational design which was no longer primarily individual. In view of this work his insistence on artistry in 1914 must have seemed like a reversion to first principles. The excessive verbal protest is however comprehensible, since van de Velde saw Muthesius's propositions as threatening the very balance which he had established for himself, at least for the time being. The middle view for which they were both searching simply had various aspects, canonical as well as spiritual.

Sofa and chairs in theatre director Curt von Mutzenbecher's home in Wiesbaden, probably 1906

The Kunstgewerbeschule in Weimar, 1905/6

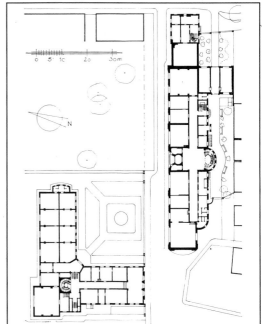

Art School Buildings in Weimar, 1904–11

The low wing of the Kunstgewerbeschule, along with the adjacent Kunstschule, was the first public commission which Henry van de Velde received. He had founded a college devoted to applied art in 1902, in order to be able to provide artistic models for the craftsmen of Thuringia. The building housed workshops, and van de Velde's studio on the upper floor.

The most striking feature of the otherwise reserved building is the gable on the street side. Its distinctive form can be interpreted in various ways. For one thing, the circular form is a particular trademark of van de Velde's. Secondly, it establishes a relationship between the light upper storey and the solid base. Thirdly, the central motif is to be seen as a pointer to the heart of the building: van de Velde's own studio was behind the gable windows (page 102).

A less than promising situation had been turned into a striking design at the stroke of a pair of compasses, as it were. The determination of this large-scale movement gives the building its character. Relatively simple accompanying forms – the severe windows, for example – ensure that the hint of extravagance is immediately brought back under control.

The outline of the slightly compressed circle is an unconscious reminder of oriental architecture. A component of van de Velde's work which hitherto had remained concealed asserts itself more clearly here than previously.

The iron lintels left visible here show another van de Velde characteristic: the emphasis on structural elements. The lintels are skilfully and convincingly linked to the stone design of the gable.

The L-shaped design of the Kunstgewerbeschule was complemented in 1911 by the long

block of the Kunstschule. Van de Velde set the two buildings in a relationship of mutual tension, based on free movement rather than confrontation. The corner at which the two buildings are closest to each other remained open, leaving space between them; the façade gable of the Kunstgewerbeschule looks past the narrow side of the Kunstschule into the open, and conversely the full width of the façade of the Kunstschule is displayed in relation to the other building. Thus the boundary of the yard is only lightly marked, allowing it to stretch effortlessly over the low stone wall to include the street in the complex.

The Kunstschule was started in 1904, but the main wing, planned from the beginning, was not added to the older section on the left until 1911. The structural idea is still faintly reminiscent of the design for the Kunstgewerbemuseum in Weimar (page 78), but detail has been visibly tightened in the mean time. The building is unmistakably architectural in concept, and any reminiscence of furniture design has been successfully eradicated. The relief-like treatment of the façades has not been lost, however. They are graduated in several layers with three-dimensional accentuation.

The emphatic contrast between the piers, with dimensions far larger than statically necessary, and the areas of glass increases the impact of the architecture without making it monumental. This is prevented above all by cutting off the pilasters in the central section; this effectively breaks the line of the building, which was intended to make an impression. The 'incomplete' solution to the design problems of this section of the building demonstrates the affront offered to traditional views by the sacrifice of the conventional gable.

View from the rear of one building towards the other

Layout of the buildings

The Kunstgewerbeschule seen from the Kunstschule, 1905/6

The Kunstschule seen from the Kunstgewerbeschule, 1904—11

Side staircase in the Kunstschule, 1911

Emphatic Verticals

The structural tendency of Henry van de Velde's early architecture is shown more tightly in a building which by its size would seem less important than the Kunstschule. The Chemnitz tennis clubhouse had to fit on to a site which was irregular in area and somewhat lacking in depth. Its impact depended on a single façade, which was all that was possible. These constraints, however, made for a very logical and precise building, with no waste: the apparently unattractive commission became a high point of van de Velde's career.

Vertical elements dominated even as early as the Weimar Kunstgewerbemuseum; they also determined the form of the Esche house to a large extent (page 81), and the Kunstschule too was articulated vertically. The same is true of the tennis club. The pier-based structure of all these buildings mirrors a basic structural tendency which makes a clear distinction between load-bearing and bridging elements. A further rule is that vertical elements are open at the top or, as in the case of the Chemnitz tennis club, only support light structures which in their turn are elongated and stretched upwards.

Similar design can also be found inside these buildings. Van de Velde even used a minor feature like the newel post on the side stairs in the Kunstschule to demonstrate the same design principle in clear yet complex fashion. The combination of a solid base with a more open, limb-like structure was a motif which was constantly repeated in his work.

Tennis club in Chemnitz, 1906–8 ▷

On the second-floor terrace

Tennis Club in Chemnitz, 1906–8

A head-on view of the front of the building shows horizontal elements largely subordinated to a dominant vertical tendency. Cornices are not continuous, but fragmented between the piers, and for the first time there is no linking roof to hold the building together visually; the top is quite flat. In the tennis club building horizontal elements have been suppressed to the extent that the wall on the extreme right has no supporting base course, and looks as though it is about to sink into the ground. It is only supported by the membrane-like tension to which the eye perceives it to be subjected. The verticality of the entire building is extended and supported by the interior design of windows, banisters and lamps.

Skeletal structure also made parts of the interior very well lit and clear. The two central fields of the second storey are open over a very great breadth, reminiscent of the design of large shops and factories. We certainly have the impression of being presented with the work of an engineer. For this reason iron sections are present to a disproportionately large extent in comparison with more solid concrete and stone.

Interior and furniture design were also on a par with the tight exterior, as shown by a comparison of the terrace chairs with the lamps.

Main façade of the building

Club-room on the first floor

In the club-room

Tennis Club in Chemnitz, 1906–8

The purpose of the building suggested that at least parts of it should be white, which suited van de Velde's liking for a high-gloss finish. On the whole his interiors had become lighter and calmer in the early Weimar years; formal exaggeration had subsided. The linking element was now the austere functionality of all the objects, and thus their inward rather than outward relationship; it is not surprising that most of them had something of a sporting note. One element in their design is the knowledge that the simplest solution may well be the most elegant. Thus it was possible to fit the bar, a seating area and a flight of steps into a very small space without too much trouble. The shelf units built into the frames of the bar are particularly successful.

Club-room on the first floor

Committee room

Committee room on the second floor

Tennis Club in Chemnitz, 1906–8

This room in the upper storey was cabin-like and intimate, functional like the hall below but darker in tone. The effect is thus heavier, but no less convincing. Notable features are the design of the desk, the economic line of the chairs and the structural articulation of the ceiling lamp. Small metal gratings admitted air to the cavities behind the wall panelling. The formal restraint, which in its day must have been more than unusual, was the result of great concentration: the rhetorically based design of van de Velde's early work had developed into a pragmatic approach which produced no waste.

The ceramic items in the room had been designed by van de Velde for mass production by the firm of Höhr/Grenzhausen. The ceiling lamp is a variation of the model on page 29.

Items from a set of silver cutlery, 1912

Heightened Functionality

Principles which had matured as part of van de Velde's architectural development can now be seen transferred back to the sphere from which they had originally been derived, that of interior design. This dining-room was part of a refurbishment scheme in a large country house and seems like a companion piece to the tennis club building, to which it is structurally similar.

The most immediately striking feature is the clear linear structure of the room. A thoughtful arrangement of slender strips almost like bars breaks it up, dividing the walls into fields of unequal size, narrow in the corners and becoming broader towards the centre. This created considerable tension: the articulation corresponds with the dynamic of the walls themselves, which naturally increase in importance towards the middle, and it also increases the impact of the corners by tightening the rhythm. The room would have been much less lively if the fields had all been the same size. More attention was drawn to the corners by setting the panels into them. Their diagonal arrangement allows the rhythm to run from one wall to the next, creating a continuity of movement embracing the whole room.

The wall strips did not simply serve to articulate the room, however, but also held the wall covering. This was made clear by small metal tongues protruding into the fields; in the same way the metal bands on the edge of the ceiling are intended to link the lower section of the ceiling with the plastered area.

The sideboard is the principal feature of the room, which is fairly large and needed a focal point of this kind. The sideboard has an architectural look: a broad central section is flanked by two rounded side pieces which could be turned to open them up. A link to the wall behind is provided by four diagonally placed drawers which swivelled, and could all be locked with the same strip of wood.

The cutlery is among the very few applied art designs produced by van de Velde in his late Weimar years. Its precise lines corresponded with those of the buildings and rooms contemporary with it.

Dining-room in Arnold Esche's house in Lauterbach/Thuringia, 1907/8 (see also page 104)

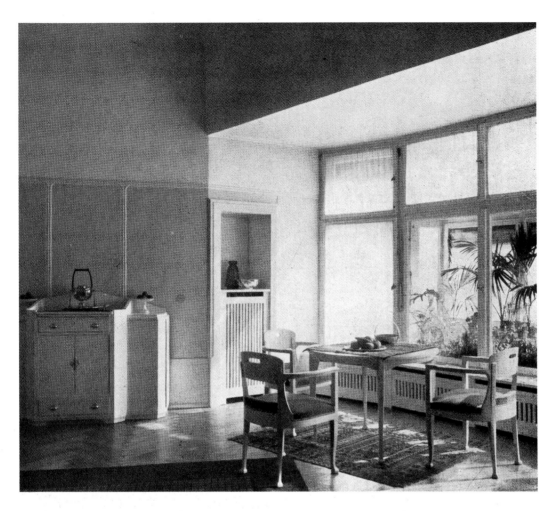

Bay in the painter Curt Herrmann's Berlin residence, 1910

Severity and Tension

At first sight this doctor's town house seems almost unassuming. Lack of space prevented expansion on all sides, and the architectural effect had to be made using two visible sides only.

The street side was suitably disciplined for its situation, but not symmetrically designed. The axes are slightly displaced, the window proportions change, and other differentiation meant that the austerity carried a certain tension within it. Thus the bay was not central, but shifted slightly to the right, and this asymmetrical weighting was compensated for by displacing the entrance slightly to the left. It therefore looked as though it had been cut out of the lower part of the protruding section, and provided an upbeat for the modelling of the façade. The bay itself joins

the façade at an angle of 45 degrees and thus retained contact with it. Upper storey and roof of the bay are covered with slate, fitted like a medieval chain helmet, into which van de Velde incorporated the roof spandrels with particular skill. The top of the bay is semi-circular, and thus almost supple; in fact the severe forms of the lower part of the house are compensated for in the upper part of the building, as can also be seen in the attic window.

The idea behind the interior of the Hermann residence, which contains one of Henry van de Velde's most beautiful white dining rooms, is similarly lucid to the one on which the house is based.

Fröse house in Hanover, 1910 ▷

Intimacy and Public Show

The picture on page 129 shows a rather faint figure in the right foreground which is probably Henry van de Velde. If that is indeed so, he is looking at his own house at the moment of its completion – it is still without the creepers which can be seen in later photographs. The scene is striking in its intimacy: a longing seems to have been fulfilled; beyond the clearing is the house which after Bloemenwerf was the second haven he had created for himself. Given the size of the family, the surprisingly meagre scale of the building makes clear the extent to which it was intended as a protective covering, a characteristic confirmed by the architectural details of the roof, the sunken loggias and the solid masonry.

Even though van de Velde was entitled to feel that developments up to this point in Weimar confirmed what he stood for, he in fact read the situation differently. Some of his hopes had been disappointed: neither the planned country restaurant Im Webicht nor Louise Dumont's ambitious attempt to found a 'Bayreuth of the Theatre' in the town of Goethe had proceeded beyond the plans which van de Velde had prepared. The Kunstgewerbemuseum was also to have been developed on a much larger scale, but neither that nor the extremely detailed suggestions for the rebuilding of the existing museum were executed. Only the first stage of the Kunstschule (built from 1904) and the small Kunstgewerbeschule building dating from 1905/6 were eventually built, and the same is true of the Chemnitz tennis clubhouse of 1906–8. Other attempts to work outside Weimar – the museum hall for the great Dresden 'Kunstgewerbe' exhibition in 1906 and the hoped-for commission to design the interior of an ocean liner for the shipbuilder Albert Ballin – were failures or fell through. The latter project remained unrealized ostensibly because of an objection by Kaiser Wilhelm, who had expressed his displeasure at an interior by van de Velde with the prescient remark that he did not wish to be made seasick. In fact designing a ship would have suited van de Velde's inclinations and abilities extremely well: the 'Yachting Style' of his work, noticed at his first appearance in Paris, predestined him for such a commission. He must have been particularly hurt by the loss, as many of his German colleagues – Olbrich, Riemerschmid, Paul and Troost, for example – had been successful in this field with relatively conventional designs. He was thus denied the great commission which would have suited him so well.

As before, only private commissions could help him over this unsatisfactory situation, so injurious to his personal pride. A very successful example is the interior of Esche's house in Lauterbach. There then follow the rooms presented by van de Velde, along with the museum hall, in Dresden in 1906, the interior for Curt Herrmann and some other examples, in all of which the high-gloss furniture is outstanding. This surface treatment always drew corresponding strictness of design from van de Velde, and new technology made possible a basic structure which gave scope for the simplicity which the artist had probably had in mind for some time. He could now abandon the traditional frame and panel technique.

In 1907/8 van de Velde built his own house Hohe Pappeln in Weimar and the Hohenhof in Hagen for Karl Ernst Osthaus. In 1910/11 he built houses for Rudolf Springmann in Hagen and Aderhold Fröse in Hanover. He journeyed to Riga to plan a priest's residence and school building.

Theatre in Weimar, pages 85 and 89
Museum in Weimar, page 78
Tennis club, pages 113–19
Kunstschule in Weimar, pages 110–12
Museum hall in Dresden, page 67

Page 124: Henry van de Velde with his family outside his home, Hohe Pappeln in Weimar, c. 1910

Karl Ernst Osthaus, painted by Ida Gerhardi in front of a set of shelves in the Folkwang-Museum, 1901

All these interiors enjoy great certainty: they are disciplined, precise, functional and give the impression of being of the greatest possible use to their owners. They almost all show the same mastery as the interior of the tennis club. In their precision, almost that of a model – it is conceivable that some of the furniture could have been mass produced – they are superior to the highly individual style of the designs for Graf Kessler in the early Weimar period.

If at this period Graf Kessler was the friend who advised, warned, made sensible judgments in artistic matters, and was generally helpful, supportive and persuasive, then Karl Ernst Osthaus was a demanding promoter, who asked more and achieved more. He made very firm judgments, but also accepted guidance once he had recognized the necessity for it. This had happened in 1900, when van de Velde persuaded him at their first meeting to extend the planned Folkwang-Museum beyond the existing scientific collection and to make it a home of modern art. In his biography of the artist, Osthaus frankly reports that he had not originally intended to use van de Velde as the architect for his own house, but that the architect's more recent work had persuaded him to offer the commission after all. Osthaus seems to have had no feeling of obligation to van de Velde, and the choice was quite freely made.

The projected building, the Hohenhof, was a mixture of urban villa and country house; urban style was combined with a lifestyle free of a sense of being under observation. On the one hand a framework for urban ceremony was provided, suitable for artistic presentations and in which the lady of the house wore gowns and jewelry designed by the architect; on the other hand, by means of axes, terraces and viewpoints it was possible to admire the charming country setting from all angles, and the complete design included greenhouses and a dovecot by the entrance as well as several garages, pools and spacious garden terraces.

The principal work of art outdoors was a figure by the exuberantly physical sculptor Aristide Maillol, and it was voluptuously supported in the interior by tile pictures featuring nudes by Henri Matisse. Osthaus had both of these placed near to his study. The picture *The Chosen One* by Ferdinand Hodler made a rather more austere impression; this awaited the visitor in a niche in the hall after he had been greeted by two nude reliefs by Hermann Haller on either side of the front door. Finally, in the drawing-room, there was a large landscape by Edouard Vuillard which dominated the wall, and a glass picture by Johan Thorn-Prikker had been incorporated in the niche behind the master of the house's writing desk. There were also various randomly arranged pictures. Works of art were indeed an important feature of the whole building, but neither Hodler nor Vuillard fared particularly well, and one suspects that van de Velde found these pictures something of a nuisance, too much competition. Everything else fitted in with his design very well.

A complex combination of urban grandeur, individual self-realization and artistic integration make the Hohenhof a *Gesamtkunstwerk*, similar to Josef Hoffmann's Villa Stoclet, which dates from the same period. Both buildings are comparable in pretension, position, size and purpose, even though the Hohenhof makes a more modest impression in comparison with the palatial villa. The Hohenhof is more tendentious than the Villa Stoclet, in the interior of which the style of the Wiener Werkstätte is very much to the fore, and other aspects, such as the owner's oriental collection, hardly fit in with the overall design. Osthaus is more recognizable as an individual in his house and his inclinations have been considered to a much larger extent. This shows not only in the interior, but in the overall architectural concept, which is strikingly firm in its direction. Despite its outward heaviness it seems to be imbued with surging movement – an impression which is easily communicated to the onlooker; he does not wish to stand looking at the house for long, but wants to walk round it, falling in with the suggestion it makes.

Another point of view is also important: while the Villa Stoclet was built by a Viennese architect for a highly cultivated Belgian patron in the cosmopolitan city of Brussels, the Hohenhof was built by a Belgian in the up-and-coming town of Hagen for a very demanding German patron, and was artistically one of the most lavish residences ever created in Germany. International movement apparently was the prerequisite of both architects if they were to produce an outstanding piece of work.

The Hohenhof was a step beyond the form of upper-middle-class residential culture current at the time, but the attempt to make it the centre of a villa colony echoed similar schemes which had preceded it – such as the Mathildenhöhe in Darmstadt. The layout designed by van de Velde for the little hill topped by the Hohenhof is similar to that of the Mathildenhöhe, but it would hardly have been possible for it to be different if the character of a loose grouping was not to be broken by undue regimentation. There were practically no attempts at innovation; at the most the appearance of the buildings themselves and the way in which they fitted together was potentially interesting.

The plan was not very successful, and only three houses were built in the immediate vicinity: the Villa Cuno turned out to be somewhat aggressive, severe and compact; the Villa Schröder was extremely austere and very regular; and finally came the Goedecke House, which is rather indifferent. They are in no way an answer to van de Velde's architecture. Only the buildings in the street called Am Stirnband, a little further away, respond to the stimulus he provided. The Dutch architect J. L. M. Lauweriks built six houses which, both in coordination and grouping, are a perfect example of the use of urban space.

They take their lead from the Hohenhof to a large extent in the use of materials, but in layout they show a freedom well ahead of their time. The Hohenhof confirmed Osthaus's confidence in his architect, and led to more contracts for van de Velde from the former's relations. Rudolf and Theodor Springmann both commissioned villas in Hagen (1910/11 and 1914/15), and Osthaus's brother-in-law, Dr Aderhold Fröse's, town house in Hanover was also built by van de Velde (1910). The two earlier works were highly successful, the later one less so. Smaller commissions came from the Colsman family, also relations of Osthaus.

Osthaus was once more able to help van de Velde on a large scale when commissions were being distributed for buildings for the 1914 Werkbund exhibition in Cologne. It was essentially thanks to Osthaus that van de Velde was allowed

Side room in the Hohenhof hall with Ferdinand Hodler's picture *The Chosen One*

Study in the Hohenhof with Johan Thorn-Prikker's later colour decoration, *c.* 1914

House for Rudolf Springmann, pages 146–47
House for Theodor Springmann, pages 26 and 167
Fröse house, page 123

Josef Hoffmann, Palais Stoclet in Brussels, garden side, 1905–11

Peter Behrens, Schröder house in Hagen, 1908/9

Peter Behrens, Cuno house in Hagen, 1908–11

Karl Ernst Osthaus, *Van de Velde, Leben und Schaffen des Künstlers*, Hagen, 1920

to build the theatre there – his principal work. Osthaus had thus shown himself to be that happy acquisition, a courageous, demanding, and above all consistent supporter.

He was also van de Velde's first biographer. The book was written in 1919 – when its subject was living without commissions in Switzerland – and published a year later, when he had already started to work for the Kröller-Müllers in Holland. Gratitude, together with a wish to help the artist when he found himself in strained circumstances, may have prompted Osthaus to make his début as an author, albeit one who did not formulate very thoughtfully. All his assessments, even critical ones, were essentially honest, but the author's obsessions tend to intervene. Several attacks on Jewish businessmen with whom van de Velde was associated for a time give the impression that Osthaus saw the artist almost as a commodity which he had bought on the stock market, negotiable only through him. He was very much at home with economic thinking – when it was a matter of obtaining commissions for Hagen craftsmen, for example. Furthermore, van de Velde, as a Fleming, seemed to represent a racial guarantee against Levantine abominations. Such phenomena blur the picture, but at least make it free of idealistic fog.

J. L. M. Lauweriks, row of houses in Am Stirn- band street in Hagen, 1912

Hohe Pappeln in Weimar, 1907/8

Entrance side with study windows

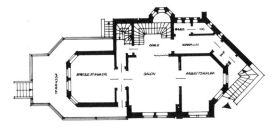

Plan of the ground floor

Hohe Pappeln in Weimar, 1907/8

Hohe Pappeln was the second house which van de Velde built for himself and his family. It is clearly related to the Bloemenwerf house, although the details differ. In each case the character of a modest country or garden house is emphasized, in contrast with the usual villa style. In the new house too the design of the roof controls the rest of the architecture to an important extent, suggesting protection and security. This trait is even more strongly marked than before, as the roof almost completely encloses the end of the upper storey.

The polygonal ground plan is also directly reminiscent of the Bloemenwerf house. In both buildings rigid geometrical forms have been avoided in favour of bevels, curves and protrusions. The entire design is broken at a number of points, which makes it look formally more complex than its actual volume would lead one to expect. As you walk round it the house presents far more aspects than the usual four viewpoints could possibly offer. Limited space has been compensated for by complex exterior design.

In the case of Bloemenwerf the polygonal shape seemed random and not always convincing, but it is now tight and controlled. This shows most strikingly in the ground plan, in which the dominant longitudinal axis remains unconcealed by the polygonal shape. The house is shaped almost like a ship, but its uncompromising nature is relieved by a lack of symmetry; on one side the sequence of entrance, anterooms and hall opens out of the central section containing dining-room, living-room and study. This arrangement is unusual, as the main and side axes do not cross, but run parallel with each other. It is only in the main hall that a broad opening establishes a connection. The interior organization is first discerned from the 'bow', which means that this feature is particularly accentuated, even though the thrust then changes from the main to the side axis. Despite the numerous protrusions the ground plan never seems confusing, each break occurring at an angle of 45 degrees.

This confidence was not maintained in the exterior, where many transitions seem harsh and abrupt. This is particularly true of the bay on the long side, which does not fit in on the left hand at all; it is little better on the right. The roof over the entrance, however, is all the more convincing. Here the intersection of the polygonal run of the walls, the rising diagonal of the stairs and the double break in the roof make a considerable three-dimensional effect. The inset arrangement of the entrance makes a pleasing contrast with the thrusting form of the roof.

The garden side with – from the left – dining-room, drawing-room and study on the ground floor

Rear of the house from further away

Hall and staircase

Hohe Pappeln in Weimar, 1907/8

The intimate look of the exterior, designed for family life and not to make an impression, is continued in the interior. The hall is modest in dimension, but extended by a bay window and the broad opening to the drawing-room. The two rooms are interconnected, and the dimensions increase from the bay window via the hall to the large room, in a sense conducting the visitor through the flight of rooms from the point of entry on the right. The nature of the furniture both extends and transforms the role of the staircase area as the point of access to the upper storey: the space looks extremely lived-in and is obviously the heart of the house. The light design of the stairs makes a fundamental contribution to the pleasingly informal mood of this part of the house. The character of the whole building and of individual pieces of furniture is reminiscent of those designed for Harry Graf Kessler (pages 95–101). This effect is not achieved without due preparation. The little anteroom directly behind the front door is surprisingly lavish in articulation despite its modest size, and its wooden structure is reminiscent of the interior of a ship. It communicates the credo of the owner of the house in compressed form. It is unfortunately impossible to capture this room in a photograph.

The three sofas in the drawing-room, along with a grand piano and Mme van de Velde's desk, are older than the rest of the furniture. They came from a flat which van de Velde had previously occupied in Weimar. The picture over the sofa in the hall is by the Belgian painter Théo van Rysselberghe, and shows Mme van de Velde with three of her children. The figure under the stairs is by Georges Minne.

Drawing-room with opening to the hall and staircase

Fireplace in the study

Hohe Pappeln in Weimar, 1907/8

This is the room used by Henry van de Velde at the time when his work was reaching both a high point and a crisis. The sheltering, enclosing feel of the interior gives a good idea of its owner's way of life. This was a room designed to protect.

The basic shape is octagonal, but only half of this shape survived; the other part of the room was extended. The polygonal end of the building contains the three principal rooms in soft and supple fashion, but it is broken off somewhat abruptly by a large partition wall.

The axis of the room runs through the left-hand window of the two in the illustration. Two desks are arranged symmetrically on either side of it; they fit into the room very unobtrusively, almost melting into the other fitted furniture.

Various details are important. The sweeping elegance of the armchair is one of van de Velde's earliest designs, dating from 1898 (page 51). The chair is the same pattern as the one in the barrister Dr Wittern's consulting room (page 71). The two small lamps on the writing desks are also very early, and the same is probably true of the graceful base for the globe.

The bronze head of van de Velde in the foreground is by the Berlin sculptor Georg Kolbe, made in 1913 for its subject's fiftieth birthday, which means that the photograph must date from a few years after the room was originally furnished. The second bronze head in the background is an older portrait by Constantin Meunier (page 46).

The fireplace is supported at the side by two wooden pedestals, and the mantelshelf is slightly raised by small supports like flattened spheres to protect it from the heat. The objects arranged on it and also those on the shelves were obviously among van de Velde's most personal possessions.

Study

Fireplace corner in the study

View from the pergola into the garden courtyard

West side

End of the side wing

North-east corner of the house

The Hohenhof in Hagen, 1907/8

Henry van de Velde built the Hohenhof for his patron Karl Ernst Osthaus at roughly the same time as he built Hohe Pappeln for himself. The villa was originally intended to form the centre of an estate, but only three neighbouring houses by Peter Behrens were built.

It is clear that one of the Hohenhof's functions is to be an articulating core at the centre of a larger group of buildings. The house is given considerable weight by its extent and materials, which make it look dominating; at the same time the building is formally extremely varied, creating many different links with its environment. Many axes originate from it and extend into the surrounding area, imposing a structure upon it.

Thus numerous dynamic factors determine the architecture of the building. As is the case with Hohe Pappeln, the Hohenhof presents a wealth of different facets which encourage the onlooker to walk around it. When one does this it is clear that every section is perfectly conceived and executed, and no single detail seems imprecise.

Particular care was exercised in the selection of materials. The basic one was a very hard, bluish-black stone quarried in the area. Where detailed work was needed it was complemented with basalt lava. Local tradition required the use of slate for covering timber frames and green paint for shutters, and both were adopted for the upper storey.

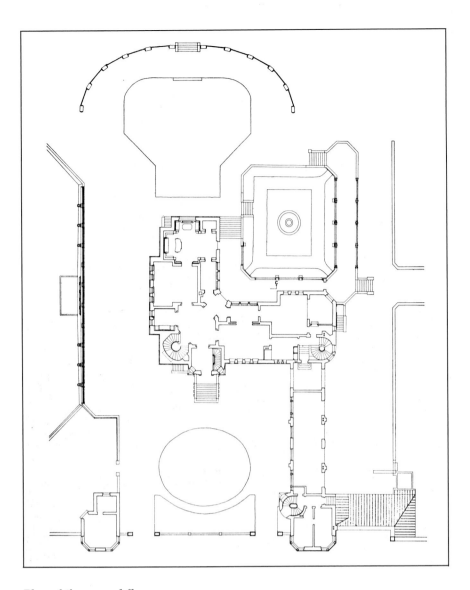

Plan of the ground floor

The Hohenhof in Hagen, 1907/8

The ground plan is a double L-shape with the main section making up the two-storey dwelling house, continued to the street by the side wing. This created two courtyards. The one in front of the entrance is further bordered by a free-standing dovecot; the other is contained within the L of the main building. On the east side the ground slopes down into the Donnerkuhle, a geographical feature to which the architecture relates. This trough is contained by a stepped bulwark on one side and included in the composition. At the same time the only symmetrical façade of the house faces in this direction. This is a stabilizing feature within a very complex system of buildings.

The garden court, intended for private use by the family, is behind the east wing, which completely faces the view on the valley side. This pattern means that the south side of the house does not have a 'face' of its own, but is divided into two separate views, which complement each other beautifully. This is true of the articulation as a whole, as well as the detail. The displacement of the windows in the ground floor bays is balanced, and the diagonal run of the two segments of wall which detach themselves from the body of the house in the same way gives parallel alignment to the front and rear sections of the south side. This orientation is strengthened by the terrace which forms the western end of the sunken garden court. An axial relationship, better understood from inside the house, extends from the south window of the study past Aristide Maillol's sculpture *Serenity* and a pergola forming a half-oval to a short avenue.

The house itself is based on a very intelligent ground plan. Parallel to the outer sections containing the main rooms a conservatory, divided into three, connects the more distant rooms to the central hall at the inner constricted point.

South side of the Hohenhof with Aristide Maillol's sculpture *Serenity*

East side from further away

View into the hall from the stairs

Hall with view of the staircase

The Hohenhof in Hagen, 1907/8

The hexagonal form of the hall came about because of the displacement of axes between the
entrance and the sequence of drawing-room and
study. Over a long distance the space forms a link
within the series of major rooms, and over a short
distance it connects the conservatory with the
staircase in the upper storey. This creates an axis
which runs diagonally and thus sets off in a new
direction. It extends through the inner section of
the house into the garden court – although it does
have a somewhat indistinct course, as it is slightly diverted by the rectangular form of the court.

Both views of the hall were taken across this
diagonal axis, one with a view into the circular
stair-well, and the other from the foot of the steps

back into the hall and the gallery-like conservatory. These doorways are higher than the others,
and so stand out. The space for the stairs themselves is of relatively small dimensions; apparently the point was to be made that it was only
for private use. To the right of it is a small square
room intended as a waiting-room for visitors.
The wall opposite the sofa was taken up almost
completely by Ferdinand Hodler's picture *The
Chosen One* (page 127).

The light fittings are particularly well integrated: they are set on wooden pillars on either
side of the doorways. The spatial diversity of the
hall is surprising, regardless of the angle from
which it is viewed.

Niche in the Hohenhof study, with desk (see also page 127)

Dining-room (see also page 23)

One of the two sideboards in the dining-room

Drawing-room

The Hohenhof in Hagen, 1907/8

The drawing-room was built around Edouard Vuillard's picture *The Walk*, the colours of which van de Velde picked up in the carpet. There were pedestal mirrors on either side of the painting which underlined the slightly ceremonial atmosphere – the drawing-room was by far the most conventional of all the rooms in the house. The rather stiff sofas are arranged like those in Hohe Pappeln (page 133). The door on the left in which one of the pedestals is reflected led into Herr Osthaus's study.

The picture may have been intended as the focal point, but less for its own sake than as a decorative element. It must be said that it was handled somewhat arbitrarily: it was difficult to look at it properly because it was partially covered by one of the sofas and it is not possible to stand far enough back.

Things were more relaxed in the narrow conservatory, which led directly into the study. Here was some of the basketwork furniture which had already been used in Graf Kessler's flat (page 99). The wall picture made up of coloured tiles is an early work by Henri Matisse.

Part of the conservatory, outside the study

Pergola on the south side

Rudolf Springmann's House in Hagen, 1910/11

This house, designed by van de Velde for his relative Rudolf Springmann, was originally intended to be part of the estate planned by Karl Ernst Osthaus around the Hohenhof, but it was finally built in much-changed form on a different site. The rather narrow plot drops sharply on the north side, and so the house had to be prevented from looking as though it was going to slip away. The central building has therefore been provided with a series of complementary sections which work against this tendency. The round bay window on the street side clearly performs this function by giving the house an obvious anchorage point. The stepped sub-division of the house itself makes an effective contrast with this, making it look lower and nearer to the ground. This means that the first floor has been treated like an attic storey and the roof itself looks like a hat pulled down over the eyes.

Another essential feature is that most of the formal transitions are soft and rounded, setting up a flowing movement which never ends abruptly, but is always in motion. The house looks as though it was shaped by a delicate hand capable of sensing the slightest nuance. In fact all van de Velde's buildings were first made in plaster, to test their sculptural value. The subtlety of the model which must have existed for this house was transferred to the full-scale architecture.

The essentially bold stroke of uniting the storeys within the semi-circular bay window clashes with a relatively conventional ground plan which does not prepare for this spatial situation. The breakthrough to the upper storey is not clear from the outside because the articulation of the façade remains traditional; a hint is given by the decorative bars, however.

North-west side of the house, with entrance

Temptation to Work on a Large Scale

The neat little gentleman at the door of the monument is Henry van de Velde; the architecture thus provides a measure of the physical size of its creator. He seems surprisingly small. The comparison to which van de Velde subjects himself here may be the key to the fundamental contradiction in his work, that between exterior and interior dimensions. However subtle his previous creations may have been, they were still striving towards significant form. Even an early work like the famous kidney-shaped writing desk shows this characteristic, and the tendency is also borne out in most of the objects designed after 1900. Van de Velde's work was rarely 'light', and even when this is to an extent masked by a more relaxed approach, the result is always weighty and carries the force of a model. His objects, whether we like them or not, are unlikely to meet with indifference.

Early in the second decade of the Weimar period his ability to balance interior and exterior dimensions began to wane, and his designs became strikingly monumental. This was not entirely unheralded, but its intensity is nevertheless surprising. It is as though a dam which had held for some time had suddenly given way.

This explanation is based on van de Velde's temperament; the theory can also be supported by an analysis of circumstances at the time, allowing for contemporary tendencies. There is no doubt that much which had previously been suppressed now emerged in the larger commissions he received. Monuments, a large theatre and, equally important, a museum were the kind of task with which he would not hitherto have been entrusted. Their importance cannot be ignored, and they brought him artistic recognition which may have left the 'engineer' in him unmoved, but affected the creative human deeply. Even at his most disciplined, the premises on which all his work was based were never suppressed to the extent that the artist in him was silenced. That artist was only satisfied with the possibility of creating 'absolute form'. Monument, theatre and museum were most suited to this. As a test for van de Velde – if he did not wish to betray his own principles – they were practically essential.

This attitude apparently also dictated the character of the commissions – there is no record that van de Velde was offered other monumental projects, administrative buildings, embassies, exhibition halls or factories, for example. It was simply and solely – or rather precisely – buildings concerned with art which were entrusted to him. The tragedy was that he had an understandable desire to move in a particular direction, but a satisfactory solution had become almost impossible. The reasons for this are many and various, and also interlinked.

Firstly, the opportunity came too late: van de Velde was too old for this sort of work, and had been worn down by waiting for it too long. Suffering and doubt were poor bases on which to build important achievements. Peter Behrens, who was roughly the same age and also a self-taught architect, had been given his greatest commissions much earlier, when he still had the necessary strength. Van de Velde was also going through a period in which friends like Bodenhausen

In 1909–11 the Abbe memorial was built in Jena. In 1910/11 plans were made for the Théâtre des Champs-Elysées in Paris, and in 1911/12 designs for a Nietzsche stadium in Weimar. The Dürckheim and Henneberg villas were built in Weimar in 1912/13, and villas for Körner in Chemnitz and Schulenburg in Gera in 1913/14. In 1914/15 came the villa for Theodor Springmann. The year 1913/14 saw designs for a museum in Erfurt, and 1914, building of the theatre at the Deutscher Werkbund exhibition in Cologne. From 1921 to 1926 van de Velde worked on a commission for the Kröller-Müller family in Hoenderloo and various premises for firms. In 1920/21 he built his own house, De Tent, in Wassenaar near The Hague. In 1926 he made designs for buildings on the left bank of the Schelde in Antwerp.

Page 148: Henry van de Velde in front of his monument to the physicist and social politician Ernst Abbe in Jena, probably 1911

Silver tableware (c. 1910), an example of the tendency to the monumental in van de Velde's later applied-art work

The Henneberg (1913) and Dürckheim (1912) villas in Weimar

and Kessler were increasingly withdrawing the protection which they had hitherto afforded him. It was a natural process: relationships changed and he was granted increasing independence. Corrections of the kind that Eberhard von Bodenhausen was particularly good at formulating are likely to have been less frequent in this period – no doubt this was a perceptible turning-point.

Secondly, the massive quality which now characterized his work was in essence contradictory to van de Velde's talent. Hitherto his strength had been his ability to imbue material with energy, to permeate it formally and spiritually. His best work is transparent, articulated, supple and seems to be filled with pulsating life. Thus large, weighty forms were a betrayal of his most personal abilities, a devaluation of his gifts. There is an existential explanation for this: it would appear that the possibility of, just for once, showing oneself to be 'lavish' is a temptation for all artists; it is a particular phase in their work, and can only be avoided with effort. It is usually associated with great success, as increased material size almost automatically brings weightier appreciation – at least temporarily.

Thirdly, the period in which van de Velde made his bid to work on a larger scale was not favourable. The final years of the Wilhelmine era had created a period style which was strikingly insensitive, boastful and petrified. Characteristic of the epoch are Bismarck towers and similar monuments, undisguised statements of wealth and power. Van de Velde had to accommodate himself to this trend if he did not wish to remain on an aesthetic and esoteric plane. Thus at this time not only his larger designs incline to the monumental, but villas, book bindings and tableware show a similar tendency. These objects will certainly have been appreciated by clients who ordered them, however.

It is the domestic buildings, of which van de Velde built a surprisingly large number at this period, which show that the trend towards the monumental was not a fleeting error, but a conscious intention. The villas and their interiors do not give us the impression that van de Velde was indifferent to the commissions. They were thought through with extraordinary care, and very precise in detail.

This could also be due to the fact that the three major projects were never realized, despite extensive preparatory work. Intrigue prevented van de Velde from completing the Théâtre des Champs-Elysées; the Nietzsche stadium foundered as a result of financial difficulties; and the plan for a museum in Erfurt was halted by the First World War. Only the monument for Ernst Abbe was built, from 1909 to 1911, small in its dimensions but ambitious in design. As it was actually built, rather than abandoned at the planning stage, it is possible to use it to examine van de Velde's ideas on compact design. Sculptor and engineer here seek to complement each other symbiotically: there is no doubt that the overall design was conceived sculpturally, and likewise most of the details; the interior articulation of the outer wall panels on the other hand shows an intention to simulate piercing of the walls. This effect is superfluous and without point, however, as the idea of hinting at openings here is in conflict with the interior design: the walls are clad with Constantin Meunier's bronze reliefs, which demand compactness.

Model of the Groot Haesebroek house, 1921, designed for the Kröller-Müller family in Wassenaar, Holland; it still has features quite similar to those of the later pre-war villas

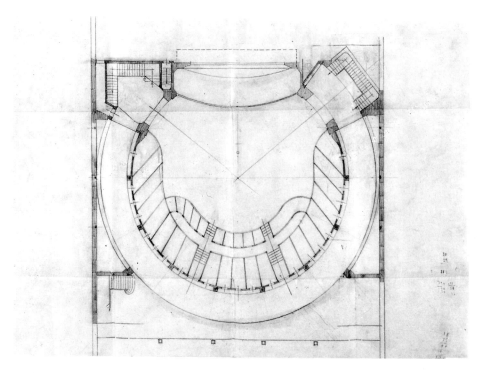

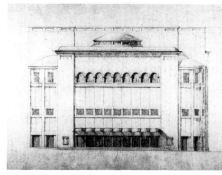

Design for the façade of the Théâtre des Champs-Elysées in Paris, 1911

Ground-plan sketch for the Théâtre des Champs-Elysées in Paris with open staircases at the side of the stage, 1911

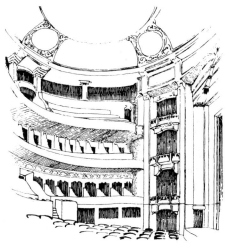

Sketch of the interior of the Théâtre des Champs-Elysées, 1911

The sketches for the façades of the Théâtre des Champs-Elysées also looked like sculptural exercises at first, but later gained a more structural thrust. All the planning for this project gives the impression of a constant struggle between these two tendencies – in essence van de Velde's persisting artistic problem. For a time he aimed for what seemed a promising balance – certain versions have the character of engineering, and yet are not without powerful formal grasp. Compared with these, the final stages seem formal and academic.

Though the sketches for the façades are clearly the work of van de Velde, the story of the design of the Théâtre des Champs-Elysées remains unclear, despite numerous publications on the subject. The project was laden with imponderables from the outset, but site, occasion and scope must have induced van de Velde to become involved. His commission – if there ever was a definite one – could only have been possible, according to Osthaus, through a front man in Paris, the architect Roger Bouvard. Probably the basic design is van de Velde's, but the uncertainty of his position, lack of experience of a project of this size and the fact that, despite having a Paris studio, he was not able to be on the spot all the time, presumably led to the contract finally being awarded to the proven Parisian architect Auguste Perret. The crowded ground plans – the very long, narrow site had to accommodate a large and a small theatre and a gallery – nevertheless contain one idea which bears van de Velde's stamp: two staircases at the side of the stage doorway open on to the auditorium like boxes, giving a diagonal view of the space. The audience in the galleries can be seen on their way up the stairs – an unusual and socially attractive perspective. It also made surprisingly original use of otherwise dead space within a rounded auditorium. The idea was later destroyed when Perret extended the galleries to the proscenium arch in order to fit in a few extra seats. The open boxes became plain doors.

A common affinity with Friedrich Nietzsche was probably the basis of the ambitious project which Harry Graf Kessler intended to realize with van de Velde's help. Nietzsche's name was certainly not chosen by chance; on the contrary it illuminates the entire thrust of the plans under discussion. Nietzsche's philosophy, as then understood, was a stimulus for van de Velde's understanding of himself. The status which Nietzsche assigned to the artist in society must have supported his own thinking. For this reason he occupied himself with Nietzsche on a number of levels – not only did he read him exhaustively, but he

Théâtre des Champs-Elysées in Paris, sketch of the façade in Auguste Perret's final version

Théâtre des Champs-Elysées in Paris, ground plans of the main auditorium (with foyer) and the dress circle (with the second, smaller auditorium) in van de Velde's version, 1910/11, cloakrooms in restricted space and a yard to service the stage

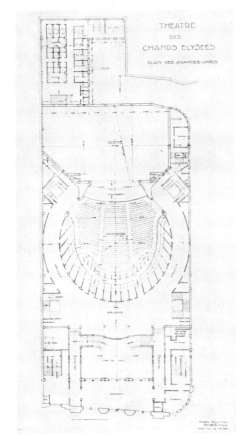 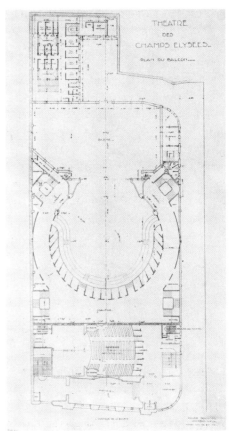

also produced designs for several of his books – some of these were sensitive and empathetic, some overloaded in a manner characteristic of the level of his understanding. Friedrich Nietzsche's sister, who lived in Weimar, had also commissioned van de Velde to design the interior of the archive containing Nietzsche's written estate, which she administered. This resulted in one of van de Velde's best works of the period: totally lacking in drama, the tone is perfectly achieved and the design gives an impression of timelessness. His approach to Nietzsche could be very subtle.

Little of this is evident in the designs for the stadium. They seem to be based on one long misunderstanding. The thunderous tone which the various versions have in common shows that on this occasion Nietzsche was to be approached in an almost violent manner. The earnestness with which this project was apparently pursued throws light on the spiritual change which had taken place within the space of ten years or so in van de Velde's Weimar circle – and certainly in the architect himself as well. The puffed-up appearance of the final work, its husk-like character, seem so artificial that we can assume that this phase in van de Velde's work would not have lasted long even if the First World War had not broken out.

Independently of the upheavals caused by the events of 1914–18, large-scale work remained a problem for van de Velde. It was still unsolved when he went to Switzerland in 1917, and there was a danger that the Weimar period – and ideed his entire life up until then – would culminate in this single point. It must have seemed a justification of all his expectations when Anton and Helene Kröller-Müller commissioned him to build a museum for their private collection in Holland. Another piece of architecture associated with art, and this time in a particularly extensive form! It was understandable if all his doubts and reservations faded into the background as a result of this apparently fortunate turn of events. The vision was too overwhelming.

The project had a history, which shows how much was expected of it. At first the idea of accommodating the collection of modern art, including outstanding pictures by van Gogh and Seurat, in a villa with adjacent gallery had been considered. For this reason the Kröller-Müllers turned in the first place to Peter Behrens, and later to Ludwig Mies van der Rohe, but did not like their designs. The outbreak of war put an end to the idea, and in subsequent years Mrs Kröller-Müller's architectural interests were focused on the building of a hunting lodge, built for the couple by the Dutchman Hendrik Petrus Berlage on an extensive site near Arnhem. The building turned out to be remarkably dark, heavy and significant – the ground plan was in the shape of antlers enclosing St Hubert's cross. This was apparently not entirely to the taste of Mrs Kröller-Müller, but she had discharged a duty to her fellow-countryman with the commission and was now free to go in search of architects once more. Various recommendations, and sympathy with his previous achievements, finally led her to van de Velde.

In the mean time the collection, protected by Dutch neutrality and probably also extended as a result of the profit made by Kröller-Müller's firm during the war, had grown considerably. Thus the plan was formed of a separate building for the collection, not attached to the villa. This would also mean that it could be open to the public – which appealed particularly to Mrs Kröller-Müller's proselytizing zeal: she was passionately concerned with certain spheres of modern art, and thus anticipated an additional role for the building, requiring appropriate expression.

This perhaps explains the militant tone which the project now took on. Van de Velde's designs gave the impression that they housed a treasure to be defended against an uncomprehending world. This essentially contradicted Mrs Kröller-Müller's intention of bringing happiness to the people; she would have been better served with an open house, but in their enthusiasm for the cause neither architect nor patroness realized the eccentricity of the course upon which they had embarked. The mistake was the outcome of a mixture of passion and defiance. No warning note was sounded, but financial losses in the shadow of German inflation finally compelled Kröller-Müller to stop work on the building – of course in the hope of being able to start again very shortly.

On this occasion van de Velde must have been even more disappointed than before, as completion of the work was in sight. The final collapse came after many unfortunate starts had been made, and even though all those involved hoped that the scheme would be rescued, they must still have been aware that it

Hendrik Petrus Berlage, two designs for the Hoenderloo museum, 1917

King Leopold III's study in the château in Brussels, 1935

The Belgian Pavilion at the World Fair in Paris, 1937 (Henry van de Velde with J. J. Eggericx and Raphaël Verwilghen)

The Belgian Pavilion at the New York World Fair in 1939 (Henry van de Velde with Victor Bourgeois and Léon Stijnen)

Binding for the de luxe edition of Friedrich
Nietzsche's *Also sprach Zarathustra*, 1908

was not just a case of a building which was not going to see the light of day, but
the death of an entire statement of faith. Despite the pain, the affair nevertheless
carried the consolation of being on a fateful scale.

Are there grounds for vindicating him other than personal ones? When van de
Velde was working on the plans for the museum in Hoenderloo from 1921 to 1926
the modern architecture of the 1920s had not yet come into being, apart from
exceptions which carry no weight here if we are concerned to defend the designer against the reproach of clinging on to an outdated concept for too long.
Pre-war architecture had survived in many places and it was not until 1925 that
there was a real breakthrough. Neither must one forget that van de Velde was
particularly concerned to use ideas which he had so far been prevented from
realizing, and this makes the artistic aspect of the plans for the museum easier to
understand. It does not explain their monstrous scale, however.

Similar points can be made about his ideas in 1926 for buildings on the left
bank of the Schelde in Antwerp. At the time – compared for example with
American skyscraper architecture – they were entirely modern and in touch
with contemporary ideas of urban planning. Even the sensitive Harry Graf
Kessler thought they were successful and the visions of the future in the film
Metropolis may have confirmed this. The design was never realized; more cred-
ible than the two large general views is the close-up showing architectural detail.

A late satisfaction was the commission for the library in Ghent in 1936, which
came at a time when van de Velde's abilities as an architect had long since been
proven by other, better buildings. It is the only really monumental building of
his career (apart from his contributions to the World Fairs of 1937 and 1939), and
seems to make up for the prevention of all the buildings which had failed to be
built before it. But even now, despite details which have been modernized, it
represents the weaker side of its designer.

Double-page title vignette for an edition of
Friedrich Nietzsche's *Ecce Homo*, 1908

Page 155: Kötschau family tomb in Weimar,
1909

Interior of the Abbe memorial with bust by Max Klinger and reliefs by Constantin Meunier

Abbe Memorial in Jena, 1909–11

As Henry van de Velde became better known in late Wilhelmine society he was given more commissions which required monumental design. However burdensome this may have been, it did suit certain of his inclinations. A desire to express himself on a large scale had always been detectable, despite all sublimations. This can be seen in the changes to the second design for the theatre in Weimar, where the original filigree form (page 85) was succeeded by a much heavier one (page 89). The Weimar Kunstschule also turned out to be rather heavier than the earlier left-hand section suggested (page 111).

A justification for work on a monumental scale without hindrance of function came with the commission for the Abbe memorial. The only conditions to be fulfilled were that four reliefs originally created by Constantin Meunier for his *Monument to Work* had to be included, and that Max Klinger had been selected to make a bust of the co-founder of the Zeiss works. All van de Velde had to do was provide a shell.

The result was an octagonal building with two sets of four identical aspects, neutral on all sides and only orientated by the direction in which the bust is facing. From the outside the architecture

One of the four identical entrance sides

combines the three-dimensional volume of a severe basic shape with strongly differentiated individual detail. The force directed outwards is so great that at first one is unaware of the space enclosed. The most conspicuous feature is the interplay of thrusting and yielding movements on the surface. In a skilful reversal the four open sides thrust forward while the four closed ones are inset. The porticoes contrast strikingly with the walls, where the relief seems delicate when set against the force of the engaged piers and cornices. The rounded plinths which give the octagon an almost circular base are a balancing force vertically as well as horizontally. The cap-like copper roof rounds off the building with remarkable simplicity, catching and focusing the disquiet from below. In comparison with the external extravagance the interior is surprisingly unarticulated, and the concrete cavetto is particularly heavy and awkward. Only the skylight shows successful three-dimensional design.

All this dramatic activity within a confined space shows how much hitherto frustrated force flowed into this architecture. It had to support design excesses which in the last resort stand in the way of effective expression.

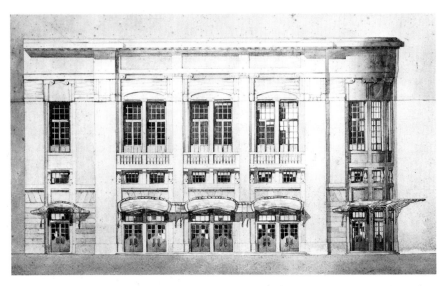

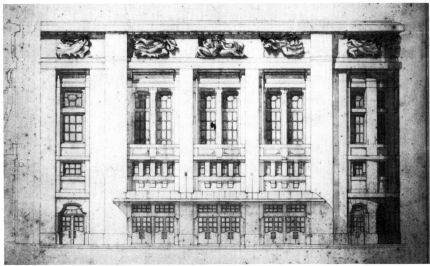

Two early versions of the façade

Middle version of the façade

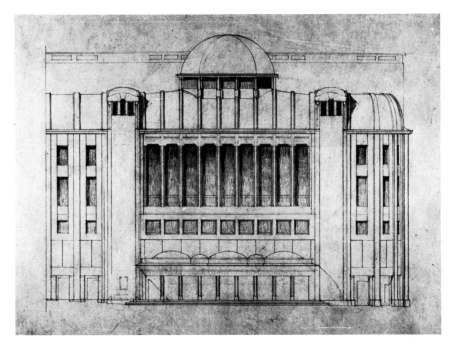

Théâtre des Champs-Elysées, Paris, 1910/11

The Théâtre des Champs-Elysées presented a further opportunity for design on a monumental scale. The commission had reached van de Velde via a private consortium hoping to use this job to make its name in France. For reasons which have still not been completely fathomed the commission was withdrawn and the French architect Auguste Perret was given the job of completing it, taking over van de Velde's ideas almost in their entirety.

In the end the building was not erected as planned in the Champs-Elysées, but in the nearby Rue Montaigne. The site was narrow and very deep and contains a foyer with stairs to the first floor, above it a small auditorium parallel to the street with separate access, a central auditorium of opera-house proportions and finally the stage and rooms serving it, set around a courtyard (page 152).

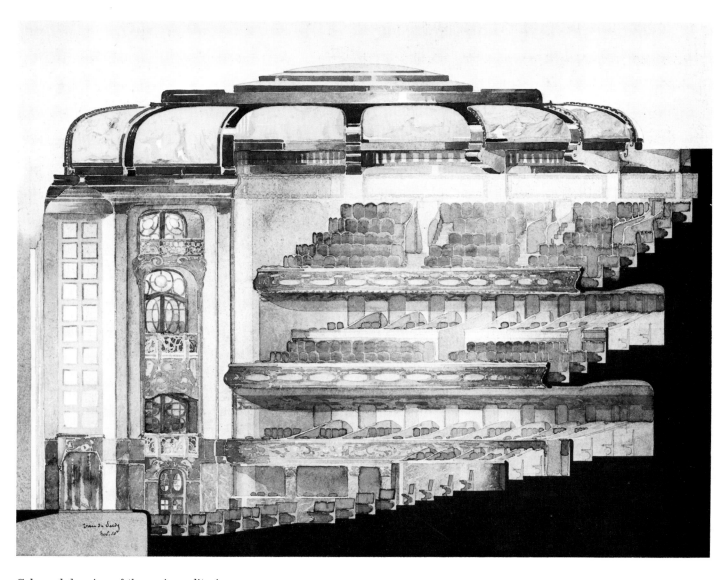

Coloured drawing of the main auditorium

Middle version of the façade

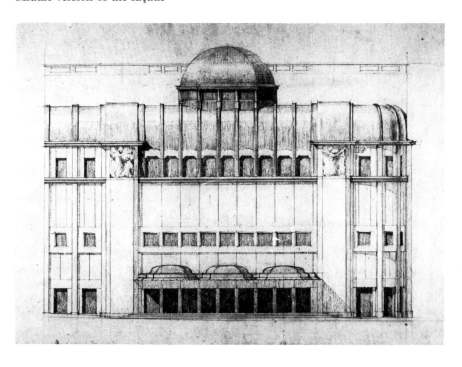

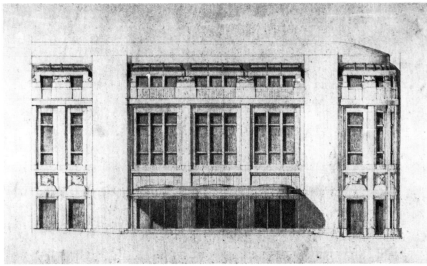

Two late versions of the façade, returning to the earliest idea

Variation of the version on page 161

Théâtre des Champs-Elysées, Paris, 1910/11

The façade design went through various stages, from the intimate via the functional to the monumental. It was a condition that Antoine Bourdelle's reliefs should be incorporated, and this was dealt with in different ways. What is probably the earliest version (see page 158, top left, probably dating from March 1911) still looks like a theatre in a holiday resort; the requirements of metropolitan architecture are not acknowledged until the second version. The design for the interior in its ornate and conservative form also corresponds to these early stages. An intermediate state can be discerned in two designs which are visibly tighter than their predecessors (pages 158 and 159 below). Emphasis on the vertical elements gives them an orientation which is further enhanced by the dome. The distinction between main and side elements has also been strengthened and the entrance and its roof are now more forceful in design. The rounded form of the roof and even more the inserted ribs make the façade look like a piece of apparatus, and convincingly cancel out the threatening monumental quality.

In two later versions this notion is abandoned and the original concept developed in purified form. It is impossible, however, to ignore the increasing weight of the architecture, and its tendency to the colossal. In the more convincing version, the main façade reliefs have been transferred to areas above the side entrances. As van de Velde already took every opportunity to

Perspective of what was probably the final version, May 1911

Variation on the above version

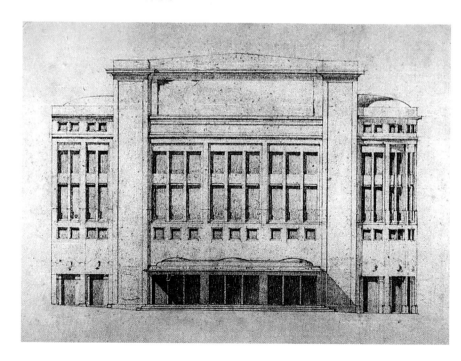

introduce three-dimensional features into his architecture, any addition was bound to be distracting.

The height of the façade was increased because of the stipulation, presumably made later, that the building should include an art gallery. In one of the later versions an upper section was added which made it look like a triumphal arch. For the first time the statuary is placed at a point which releases it from decorative subordination, but this also emphasizes that the design represents the final step from a functional-architectural concept to a monumental and dramatic one. This effect is reduced only slightly by the dead wall in the central section.

The perspective shows what is presumably the most important version (dated 22 May 1911). It is an attempt to reinstate architectural elements to the foreground. Two piers are produced above the gable and turn the horizontal trend back into a vertical one. The area intended for the frieze (omitted here) is clearly integrated into the façade. Structural features preponderate.

Perspective of what was probably the final version

Two preliminary designs

Version of the temple on a square ground plan

One side of the spectators' stands

Nietzsche Stadium in Weimar, 1911/12

After the Abbe Memorial the idea of building a similar tribute to Friedrich Nietzsche in Weimar gave van de Velde another opportunity of designing what was effectively a sculpture to walk about in. A U-shaped arena was intended, with a temple-like speakers' platform at its centre. A pool was to have formed a connecting element, with an avenue leading into the complex.

The architectural vocabulary of the various designs is similar in part to that of the Abbe Memorial. In one version van de Velde's beloved arch motif appears in the form of large openings like those in a bell tower. Rather more surprising than this version, which tends to the oriental on a square ground plan, are two ideas approximating to ancient temples. This is the first time that van de Velde turned unambiguously to historical models.

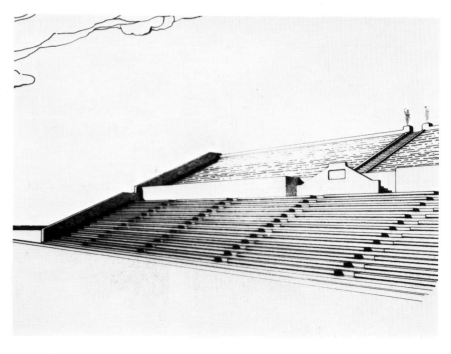

Central hall and staircase

Körner Villa in Chemnitz, 1913

In the years before the outbreak of the First World War, van de Velde received many commissions to build villas, and in some cases also to design the interior. All these houses reflect the upper-middle-class clientele who commissioned them: solid but uninspired. The particular harmony which was such a happy influence on the building of the Hohenhof does not seem to have been repeated either in the ideas or on the level of personal relationships with the clients.

What cannot be overlooked in these buildings, however, is the confusing accumulation of architectural motifs, bringing them close to the expressive monuments which van de Velde was building or designing at the same time. Massive base courses, heavy pilaster strips, cornices jutting out like slabs and heavy roofs with bulky chimneys were the dominant features in these houses, which thus looked too weighty. Again and again one can discern an intention of giving movement to the rigid, block-like basic designs by the addition of numerous detailed features, and thus to make them complicated in a way which does not stem naturally from their core. This is almost grotesque in the lodge of the Schulenburg villa, where the architecture suddenly adopts the features of a face. Essentially trivial elements were selected to express something which was no longer connected with underlying function.

Street side

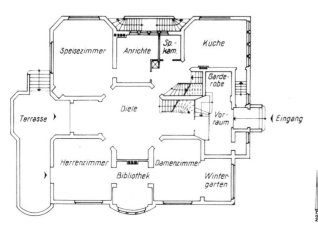

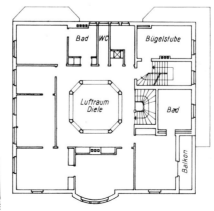

Ground plans of the two
main storeys

165

Garden side of the Schulenburg villa in Gera, 1913/14

Porter's lodge of the
Schulenburg villa

North-west corner of Theodor Springmann's villa in Hagen, 1914/15

Two Villas, 1913–15

An unmistakable learning towards monumental design became clear not just in formal detail, but also in van de Velde's fundamental decision to work increasingly to principles of centralization and symmetry. This gave added influence to a tendency which had not been dominant until this point. Early buildings and interiors had drawn attention to themselves by being symmetrical in design only where it was meaningful, but otherwise allowing free play to the balance of right and left, rather than insisting on a set form. The Hohenhof (pages 136–45) and the Fröse house (page 123) are good examples of this.

In contrast with the richness of movement found in these buildings, the later houses are petrified in design: ground plans were developed around internal halls with no sense of direction. Façades were articulated with sets of severe vertical pilaster strips and seem to be enclosed within bars. In contrast, the porter's lodge of the Schulenburg villa, with its two eyes and a nose, is strangely expressive.

Smoking-room

Dürckheim Villa in Weimar, 1912

Graf von Dürckheim-Montmartin's villa in Weimar was one of the biggest commissions given to Henry van de Velde before the outbreak of the First World War. The exterior seems un-controlled (page 150); the interior, on the other hand, is completely ossified, upper-class and pompous. While van de Velde tried to remain true to himself in matters of architecture – this is re-cognizable in the broken-up nature of the design – the interior hardly differs from contemporary Empire-style designs by Bruno Paul or Peter Behrens. It is true that the details have been handled most conscientiously, but even here routine procedures by anonymous co-workers can be detected.

Dining-room

Drawing-room in the Dürckheim villa in Weimar, 1912

Excess

Interiors increasingly lost the concentrated quality which had once been characteristic of van de Velde's best work. The rich range of motifs still has unity of line, but they look like afterthoughts, rather than organic and integrated. The impression of apparent unity rapidly breaks down into detail. It is also striking that the temperament that used to breathe such life into the work is no longer in evidence. Occasionally van de Velde's designs are so lacking in impetus that the results are conventional – his drawing-rooms look like standard rococo salons. In the example illustrated only the strange window above the fireplace provides the necessary interruption in the midst of petrified harmony.

Despite a multiplicity of external relief the design for the museum for the city of Erfurt, one of

van de Velde's last works in his German period, seems lacking in movement. One senses that the solid mass of the building has had a design imposed upon it which is neither a logical reflection of the interior, nor subject to a law of its own. The basic form is not really broken up, but only graduated. The enormous volume of the building remains the dominant feature. Furthermore the monumental cornice on the entrance façade contradicts the intention of showing that there is a courtyard at the heart of the building by pulling together the central sections of the façade. Instead the impression is given that the triumphal arch element extends throughout the building. On the other hand the exterior has too many details for the building to make an overall impact, ignoring internal differentiation.

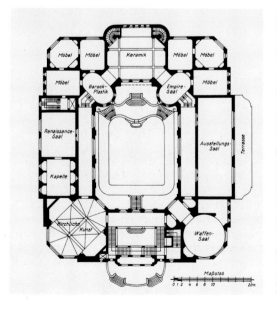

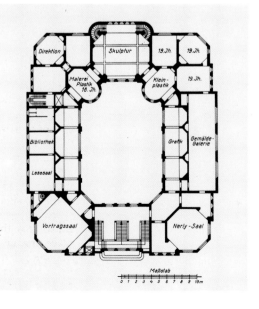

Design for a museum in
Erfurt, 1913/14; two views of
the model and ground plan
for the two principal storeys

171

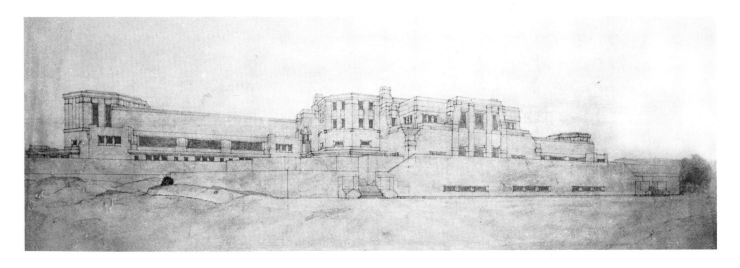

Perspective of an early version, 1921

Ground plans of the two main floors with ornamental lines, probably 1922

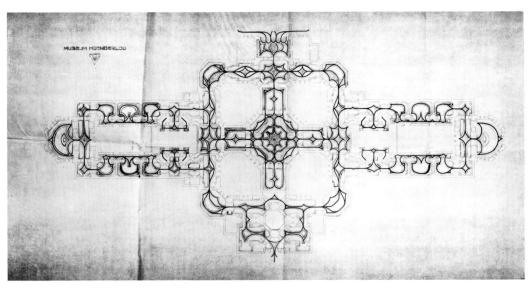

Design for the entrance, 1923

The Hoenderloo Museum, 1921–26

Henry van de Velde's major post-war project is by no means restrained, but was clearly forced unnaturally in the direction of the monumental. The Kröller-Müllers, a Dutch couple, commissioned him to build a museum for their private art collection in 1919. Van de Velde placed himself under contract to the family, and moved to Holland.

He lived there for six years, during which he completed various buildings for his new patrons and made a start on the museum, the main project, which had to be abandoned a little later for financial reasons. Only parts of the foundations were built. Before and particularly after this, the project underwent numerous metamorphoses on paper, but except in detail the basic form was never altered. The final version was fully drawn up, and theoretically it could be built and handed over for immediate use today on the basis of the surviving plans. What was actually built was a quite different version designed by van de Velde

in 1936 (pages 208–15) and intended as an 'emergency museum'.

Both Mrs Helene Kröller-Müller and Henry van de Velde became increasingly devoted to the large-scale project, the former because she saw in it the fulfilment of her artistic and pedagogic mission, and the latter because he believed that this would be his hoped-for compensation for real and imagined set-backs in Germany. The project was overblown from the beginning: it did not relate to the size and importance of the collection, nor to its surroundings. It distanced itself from both, indeed seemed hostile to them. The intention was to build the collection around relatively small pictures by Seurat and van Gogh: they would have been swamped by the architecture, and the bulwark-like appearance of the building would have been justified only with difficulty by a slight rise in the otherwise flat countryside.

Picture gallery

Director's office

Central hall

Perspective of an inner courtyard, probably 1923

The Hoenderloo Museum, 1921—26

The heart of the complex was intended to be a square block with chamfered corners, then two adjacent wings concluding in octagonal sections. The upper storey of the central section was to contain four large wells intended as a source of light for the parts of the building to the side of and below them. This created a circular gallery and a central cross enclosing as a major feature the space intended for the van Goghs. At the point where the wings began were two large double staircases, then two large rooms lit from above. These were accompanied by two storeys of small exhibition rooms. The rooms at the ends were more social in function. On the north side the walls enclosed an entrance courtyard, and on the south side steps led down to ground level. There was no independent administrative sec-

tion: the director's office was in the central part of the building.

The ground plans are a strange experiment apparently intended to show the logic and harmony of the interior by drawing in the routes taken by visitors in an almost choreographic fashion. Functional correctness asserts itself in ornamental form. Van de Velde was going back to the ideas of his early years (page 52).

The external appearance of the museum was somewhat scaled down during the six years van de Velde worked on the project, but only in detail not in overall dimensions. The spirit and intention of the project never changed; neither was the monumental design of the interior toned down. Even remote areas like the four light wells are treated with maximum architectural drama.

One of the two staircases, probably 1923

The Hoenderloo Museum, 1921–26

Even allowing for the fact that the draughtsman commissioned to draw the internal rooms was inclined to make his work excessively clear, the drawings are still congested. It is puzzling that those involved were not struck by the atmosphere of the drawings, and were not alerted to the absurdity of the whole business. The colossal stone forms of halls, staircases and galleries so dominated the impression made by the interior that the visitor would never have been prepared for the intimate dimensions of the works of art. It is symptomatic that in the illustration of the central gallery the pictures have even been robbed of their final protection – their frames.

Van de Velde's hand can only be discerned with difficulty in the design dominant here. The exterior in all its versions followed the line of development which began at the end of the Weimar period, but is scarcely true of the interior. Only details, such as the polygonal surrounds of the doorways, show hints of earlier buildings. The attitude rather than the form of the rooms is a late echo of the equally unhappy design for the museum hall in Dresden (page 67).

The central picture gallery on the upper floor, probably 1923

Entrance hall with a view of adjacent galleries, probably 1923

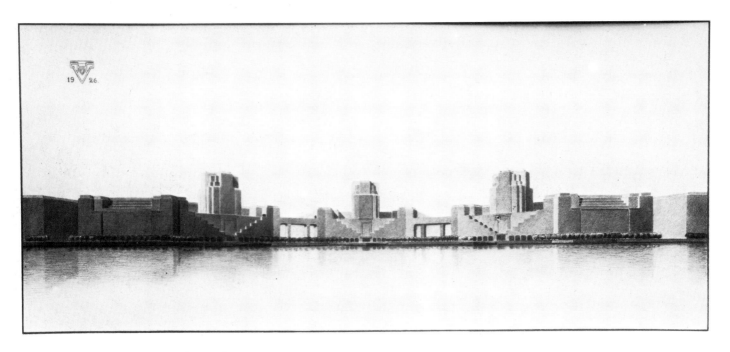

Version with double gateway and central tower

Photomontage of the planned buildings

Whm H. Müller & Co.'s travel agency in Rotterdam, 1924

Projected Scheme for the Left Bank of the Schelde in Antwerp, 1926

Designs for this urban building scheme, which added yet another new dimension to van de Velde's *œuvre*, coincided with the final version of the Kröller-Müller museum. Only drawings remain of this project; van de Velde seems to have been commissioned simply to organize the overall layout of the blocks.

The giant scale of the project may be seen in a different light today than at the time it was drawn up, when it was legitimized by other schemes, such as Le Corbusier's. Architects saw the design of large-scale buildings as a way of developing new urban environments. Van de Velde's metropolitan-style design had a utopian and visionary dimension. The stepped, offset arrangement is similar to the articulation of the museum, and it is not difficult to see the relationship of the two.

It was not until later that van de Velde came to execute large projects. He built the Belgian Pavilion at the Paris World Fair of 1937 in co-operation with architects J. J. Eggericx and Raphaël Verwilghen. The extent of these young colleagues' involvement is difficult to establish, but the relatively neutral look of the building leads one to assume that it was largely a compromise between differing approaches. The large, semi-circular form can probably be attributed to van de Velde (page 153).

Monumental design even crept into a commission as modest as the interior of the travel agency.

Version with central gateway

Variation on the version with central gateway

View of the book tower from the inner courtyard

The University Library in Ghent, 1936

About ten years after the Antwerp project Henry van de Velde received a commission for a building which was by no means on so large a scale, but comparable in every respect in terms of its demands. The University of Ghent library was designed towards the end of his career, and was the only building on a monumental scale which van de Velde was able to realize according to his own intentions.

The Antwerp riverbank scheme imposed new dimensions on the environment, and in just the same way the library tower is the dominant feature of central Ghent. Its authority is unmistakable, though the vertical articulation and the surprising formal variety of the top of the building tone it down somewhat.

The tower functions as book-stack, and stands at one corner of a tripartite building, forming a link between the reading rooms and the administrative section.

The design of the top of the tower places van de Velde's stamp on the building. It repeats the complex formal play of the Abbe monument in Jena (page 157) in more rectangular form. Even though the detail is different, the sculptural concept remains the same. The basic form is articulated by numerous backward movements, displacements and changes of direction, more penetrating in this case because of the contrast of hard and soft sections – glass against concrete. An architectural concept based on the demonstration of force reasserts itself here after a very long interval. Functions originally ascribed to line have now been finally taken over by volume.

The university library in Ghent, 1936 ▷

Permanence in Changing Times

In concentrated form the monumental phase of van de Velde's work spanned the years 1910–25, but it eventually showed signs of age and ceased to carry much conviction – yet in the midst of it there appeared the most mature building of his German period. The theatre built in 1914 for the Cologne Werkbund exhibition was an unexpected pinnacle of achievement for its time – on the one hand we find the ossification and ponderousness which has been described, then here proof of great suppleness and lightness. The contrast is confusing and scarcely explicable. Certainly many of the theatre's distinctive qualities had long been anticipated; nevertheless, architecture of this type is a remarkably isolated phenomenon within its creator's development.

This would therefore seem to confirm that van de Velde's *œuvre* had always been determined by differing tendencies – its impulsiveness could hardly spring from an equable temperament. Latterly it had inclined predominantly towards bulkiness, but it was now linked with the energy and elasticity which had been earlier hallmarks of the structural side of van de Velde's work. As is always the case with his best products, there is penetration which produces a sense of tension because the process is recognizably still alive.

Originally the theatre plan had been on a smaller scale. The 'old man' was only to build a cinema as his contribution to the exhibition. It says a good deal for the progressive outlook of the Deutscher Werkbund that its plans included such a building, but the commission looked paltry alongside the festival halls, parades of shops and terrace restaurants which other architects had been asked to design. It also meant that the site was hidden among other buildings, an addition to the courtyard of a V-shaped complex open to the rear, the so-called Farbenschau – a makeshift solution. The site determined the dimensions, and the number of seats, 450, was probably fixed as a result of this limitation. It was not difficult to foresee that the building was unlikely to make an impact.

On the other hand, the commission had its attractions because cinemas were very much a new idea at the time. There were only a few previous examples: the cinema in the Nollendorfplatz in Berlin (Oskar Kaufmann, 1912/13) was one of the first which was not built inside an older building, but rather as a separate, expensive, ambitious project. Thus there was a precedent, but one clearly influenced by previous theatre architecture, and therefore leaving numerous opportunities for extension and variation. For this reason van de Velde produced a ground plan which was fundamentally new. As a cinema does not require a deep stage or backstage apparatus, he designed a foyer which encircled the entire auditorium and thus became an enclosed passage, making it possible for patrons to circulate uninterruptedly.

The next step, a logical consequence of the first, was to turn the inner part of the building, thus released, through 180 degrees and to place the cinema screen on the entrance side. Consequently half the audience would enter from the front, with a view of the raised rear stalls. Only the last few rows had access facing the

In 1926 van de Velde returned to Brussels with official commissions: chair of architectural history at the University of Ghent and direction of the Institut Supérieur des Arts Décoratifs (ISAD) in Brussels. In subsequent years he built various villas and town houses: 1926, house for Schinckel in Hamburg; 1927, a fourth house for himself at Tervuren near Brussels, and 1929 one for Cohen in Brussels; in 1930 a country house for the Kröller-Müller family in Wassenaar, Holland, and a house for the Wolfers in Brussels; in 1931 a semi-detached house in Knokke; in 1932 a house for the de Bodts; and in 1933 a house for the Gregoires in Brussels. In 1929 he built an old people's home in Hanover and in 1932 a small clinic in Astene/Belgium; 1933/34 saw designs for two ships for the Ostende-Dover run, and interiors of carriages for the Belgian railways. In 1935 he furnished King Leopold III's study in Brussels, and in 1936 retired from official duties and built the university library in Ghent. In 1937/38 he built the Rijksmuseum Kröller-Müller in Otterlo, Holland (extended from 1940 to 1953). In 1937 with two other architects he built the Belgian pavilion at the Paris World Fair, and the same in 1939 in New York. He acted as advisor on rebuilding, 1940–45. In 1947 he moved to Switzerland, worked intensively on his memoirs, and died on 25 October 1957 in a clinic in Zurich.

Page 182: Henry van de Velde in the Dutch period, probably 1923; in the background drawings for the Hoenderloo museum

Title vignette for an edition of Friedrich Nietzsche's *Dionysos-Dithyramben*, 1914

Ground plan for the cinema design for the Deutscher Werkbund's exhibition in Cologne, 1913

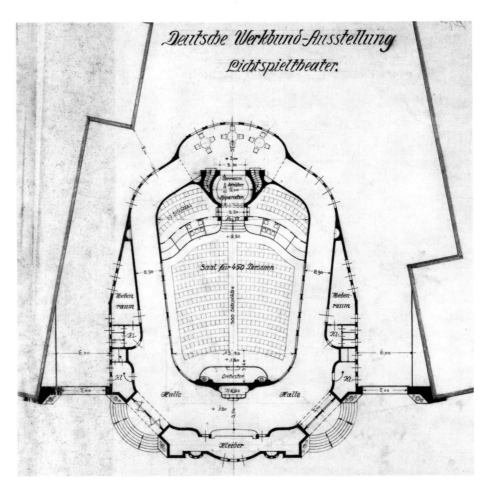

screen. This unusual device removed the original boundaries of the space, then reversed them.

It is striking how mobile, fluent and even melodious the ground plan is. There are practically no right angles, and the walls are almost always rounded, with soft lines at points of intersection. Seen as a whole the plan seems free in form, as though derived from laws of linear harmony rather than functional requirements. It is a central motif with smaller associated devices and suggests a 'stone in a setting', moving the image closer to the world of arts and crafts. The vignette designed by van de Velde in 1913/14 (at the same time as the ground plan) for an edition of Nietzsche's *Dionysos-Dithyramben* makes a very good comparison. If this design is turned upside-down, it is similar to the ground plan, not in every detail, but certainly in contour and movement. In both cases long, curving lines are juxtaposed with concentrated grammalogues, creating a state of tension. It

Ground plans of the stalls and gallery for the first version, 1913

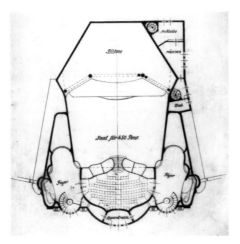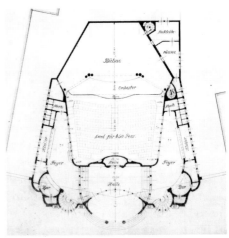

is particularly clear in the central section of the entrance side that this is architecture partially determined by highly ornamental ideas: here curved outlines of necessity enclose useless empty spaces. Pure utility would have demanded a different line. Apart from this, however, the design of the ground plan is convincing. There is no drawing of the façade, and the accompanying longitudinal section remained incomplete.

As plans for the exhibition developed, because of a change of heart on the part of the directors – or a request from van de Velde – the cinema became a theatre, with both stage and cinema projection facilities. The cramped site again caused difficulties, and the result was only a kind of studio theatre – the number of seats remained the same. Space was so limited that the rear of the raised stalls and the wall of the entrance façade almost touched.

The most striking difference from the pure cinema project was that the interior had to be turned round again and placed traditionally, in order to include a stage. Thus the plans show a transition from a lavish front section to a sober working area at the rear. This confined the ornamental treatment of spatial contours – which was retained – to the foyers and auditorium. An extremely unusual feature is the wide opening at the stage end of the auditorium: as a rule it becomes narrower at this point, but in the present case the opposite occurs. Auditorium and acting area merge, and their outline gives them the appearance of a single unit. The blending of the two spaces is only interrupted by two clusters of columns dividing the stage opening into irregular thirds: the side sections are narrower than the central one.

Here a favourite idea of van de Velde's re-emerges. The notion of increasing theatrical flexibility by allowing action to take place in several places at once had been developed during the preparation of designs for the summer theatre in Weimar. The three sections of the stage proposed by van de Velde could be used

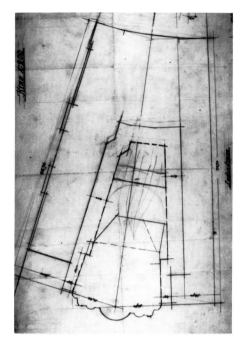

Layout sketch including extension of the plot of land, 1913

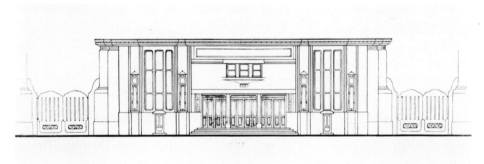

in sequence without tiresome pauses for scene changes, or simultaneously, or all as one. (It would even have been possible to remove the columns: they formed a division, but were not load-bearing.) The result would have been extremely lively theatre, and particularly useful for plays with a large number of scenes. However, this would only have been possible given the necessary space for flexible orientation of the audience – it was breadth rather than depth that was needed in the auditorium.

Provision had been made for this in the first design for the Cologne theatre, although lack of wing space would have hindered the evolution of the idea. It was evidently to remove this limitation that in the next phase the stage was considerably extended towards the rear. This was made possible because the protruding rear façade of one of the neighbouring sets of buildings had been straightened out, and so was no longer in the way.

This alteration to the ground plan introduces another innovation in addition to the rear stage: the acting area is bounded at the back by a cyclorama, which gives it a distinct outline. Parallel with this, the architecture of the entrance area

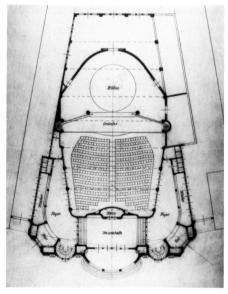

Ground plan of the stalls in the extended design, 1913

Front view of the extended version of the theatre, 1913

has also been tightened up – thus the design seems more definite, less ornamental. (The ground plan for the upper storey of this design stage is missing.)

The front view accompanying these plans seems very provisional. It gives the sense of a cinema rather than a theatre, with its (apparently) flat top, lanterns and sunken entrance, which all make the building look like a fairground booth. The effect is cheap.

The extended theatre design was now revised once more. The outline was retained but the interior articulation considerably tightened up; a structural conception replaced the ornamental one, and parallel support systems invest the plans with a pleasing sense of order. Without sacrificing any aspect of the original idea, the triad of stage, lower and upper stalls – or box-office area – here becomes a truly harmonious sequence for the first time, with a fluency of form similar to that of the cinema design. An unusual feature is that the essentially technical stage space is no exception. The apparently solid cyclorama could consequently be seen as a compositorial addition and not a necessity. However, it was retained in the later planning stages, and therefore obviously was required.

Finally, the stairs no longer go spiralling up in a corner, but are double flights on diagonal axes, clearly defining the front corners of the building and at the same time giving precise form to the foyers. The associated galleries in the upper storey were probably intended as promenades from which one could look down into the auditorium. The undulating chain of boxes between the two levels of the stalls was already a feature of the cinema design, and evidently intended to mark the break and make a more positive barrier. The accompanying longitudinal section now also shows the necessary professionalism. At this stage of the design the façade is reminiscent of its predecessor in style, but more clearly ar-

Ground plans of the stalls and gallery and front view of the third version, largely based on earlier designs, 1913

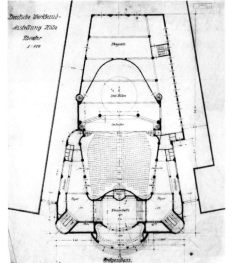

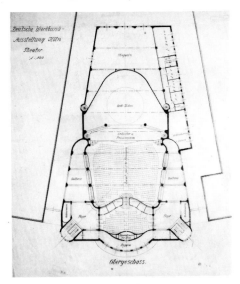

ranged. The wall areas in the central section, which as before curves outwards, are a point of rest, and the impression of something simply appended is less marked. Nevertheless, this version is not particularly inspiring either.

The decisive, liberating impulse came with the decision to remove the theatre from its cramped site between the wings of the Farbenschau and place it on a new site at the other end of the exhibition area. It was not until this point that the design was able to evolve and develop autonomous legitimacy. The individual sections of the building were rearranged in a quite different pattern. More workable storage areas at the side replaced the structure behind the stage, and the foyers were extended.

But the first plan for the new site was just an intermediate phase, combining the old auditorium design with an extended stage. The plan did not take into account a feature which now needed to be considered: an embankment in front

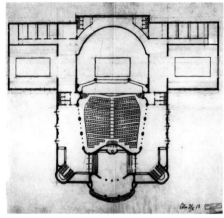

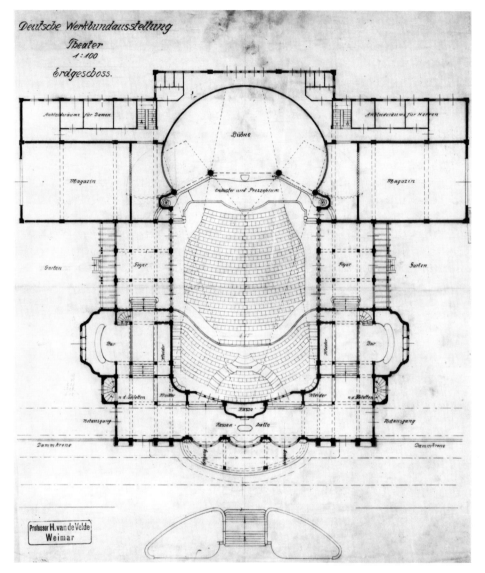

of the entrance side had to be retained. However, this complication turned out to be a helpful one, compelling van de Velde to place the entrance on a high level. Consequently the slope which he had previously had to create artificially by constructing a second storey was achieved naturally. The vestibule and the highest point of the stalls were now at the top of the rise. Thus it was possible for part of the audience to enter the auditorium directly from the back, while access from the sides ran from this point in steps parallel to the incline of the auditorium. The next – and penultimate – stage in the development of the ground plan shows this in a form which is still rather complicated. This is true of the bar space in particular. Nevertheless the situation and its exploitation were almost ideal, corresponding faintly to the layout of a Greek theatre.

Another new feature is the extension of the auditorium to provide 625 seats; the provision of cinema projection facilities had been dropped in the mean time.

Front view of the theatre at the Werkbund exhibition in Cologne, 1914

Ground plan of the final version of the theatre at the Werkbund exhibition in Cologne, 1914

Possible ways of using the divided stage, 1914

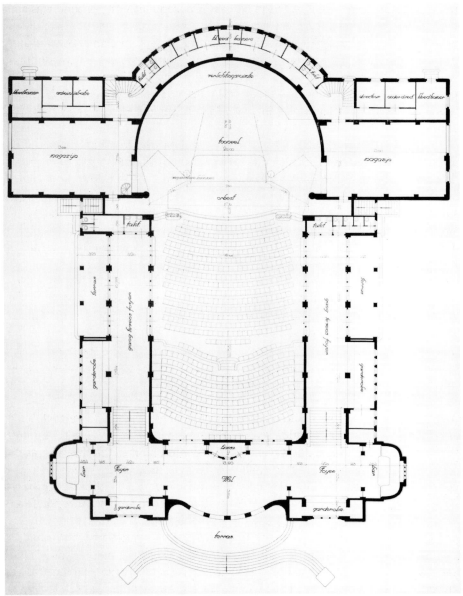

The two levels of the stalls have now been drawn more closely together, and are no longer separated by the contours of the room. The latter appears more rigid and is opened up by becoming more rectangular than trapezoid, to a lesser extent towards the stage. The concave outward curve here still corresponds to one on the rear side, but acting area and auditorium are now divided. The original fluidity has been reduced.

The last plan, the one finally built, showed this even more clearly. Nothing in the box-like space leads to the stage any longer, with the possible exception of the inevitably raked seating. The tighter structure of the ground plan is convincing, but by eliminating melodic ornamentation the original idea that auditorium and stage should melt into one is lost. The stage opening is as before divided into three, but in this form the division seems abrupt and imposed, as it in no way relates to the arrangement of the seats.

Now that the building was on a more exposed site, the exterior, hitherto limited to a narrow façade, became more important. The focus of the design was shifted, and van de Velde was no longer compelled to concentrate solely on the interior. In order to do justice to both, it was evidently necessary to sacrifice the mobile outline of the auditorium. It was becoming increasingly clear that the novel and unusual qualities of the architecture lay in precise congruity of interior and exterior design, and so the auditorium could not have been integrated in its original form, which was too restless. Consequently the outline was simplified for the sake of the overall principle. The dominant feature became the articulation of the exterior masses: supple and perfectly harmonious arrangement, and gradation and adaptation of the individual elements of the building, which almost always had the precise volume prescribed by their internal purpose. This was architecture without residual space, a building truly without waste, but it only went a small way towards fulfilling the idea of a new theatrical experience.

Essentially, however, this design also encapsulates the internal conflict of the artist, now an architect: his all-embracing notion of function clashed with fundamentally unalterable laws of aesthetic discipline. Compositorial, structural or even purely material requirements had imposed a compromise which largely succeeded with respect to architectural articulation, but did not provide the desired solution for the theatre. But in this case he came very close to the concept of a *Gesamtkunstwerk*, for which reason van de Velde constantly returned to theatre design. His vision was always a synthesis of architecture and art, but the present building was a revolutionary shell which only made limited changes to answer the demands of the theatre. If the latter requirement had been uppermost, the architecture would have suffered. It was to architecture that van de Velde – his eyes opened – owed his allegiance.

But a decision one way or the other was also necessary from the point of view of architecture – powerful innovation in the interior, so architectural history taught, was inevitably at the expense of exterior design. Van de Velde, who thought sculpturally, cared more for the latter, for which reason he relegated the interior to the background and created a particularly successful exterior – this is also true of all the other buildings for which he had been responsible up until this time. It did not mean, however, that the ground plan of the theatre was not articulated in considered fashion. The entire building is based on a system of coherently directed rectangular axes. The uncertainties of the earlier stages have all been solved – the bar space is more logically arranged; the side foyers are more lucid, though less spacious than before; and the stage area is now a precise three-quarter circle, rather than the previous indeterminate oval. The extremely complex exterior of the penultimate design is fundamentally tightened in the form which was built; the movement is taut, and the whole design gives an impression of unity. The fact that the entrance had to be raised has been used to advantage in keeping the front section of the building as low as possible, and triggers the rise which reaches its peak in the fly tower – otherwise always an evil which cannot be concealed. The forward-curving central section of the entrance side – a final reminiscence of the first designs – responds on another plane to the curve on the side slope of the gable façade. The oval windows perform a similar function. The building is dominated throughout by corresponding features. From whatever angle photographs of the building are considered, intersecting sections always provide a harmonious picture.

The only disappointing feature is the large interior, which turned out stiff and

Cologne 1914, the most important principles stated by Hermann Muthesius at the Werkbund exhibition:

1. Architecture, and with it the whole creative field of arts and crafts, strives to achieve stylization, and only by this means can it acquire once more the general significance that it enjoyed in times of cultural harmony.
2. Only with stylization, which is to be seen as the result of healthy concentration, can a generally valid, secure taste be established.

Henry van de Velde's replies to this:

1. As long as there are still artists in the arts and crafts movement and as long as they still have an influence on its fate they will make a stand against any suggestion of a canon or stylization. The inner essence of an artist is his glowing individualism, his free and spontaneous creativity, and he will never of his own free will submit to a discipline which forces him to conform to a type or canon. He instinctively mistrusts everything that could make his activity sterile, and everybody who preaches a rule that could prevent him from pursuing his thoughts to their own free conclusion, or that attempts to force him into a mould of general validity, in which he sees only a mask trying to make a virtue of incapacity.
2. Certainly an artist used to 'healthy concentration' will always realize that currents stronger than his individual will and thinking require that he recognize what corresponds essentially with the spirit of his times. These currents can be of numerous kinds, and he adopts them consciously or unsconciously as general influences, they have something materially or morally compulsive for him; he willingly subordinates himself to them and is enthusiastic about the idea of a new style for its own sake. And for twenty years many of us have been looking for forms and decorations precisely fitting for our times.

Cross-section of the final version of the theatre at the Werkbund exhibition in Cologne, 1914; the high space between the auditorium ceiling and the roof ridge may have been necessary for ventilation purposes, but probably the correspondence between internal and external volume, otherwise respected, has been abandoned here for the sake of an impressive juxtaposition of architectural forms

Erich Mendelsohn, Einstein Tower in Potsdam, 1917–21

Ground plan of a preliminary design for the Rijksmuseum Kröller-Müller which, in a much smaller and simplified form, attempts to retain the ground plan idea of the large museum in Hoenderloo, dating from 1925, when the monumental version was still under consideration

Rudolf Steiner, second Goetheanum in Dornach, 1924–28

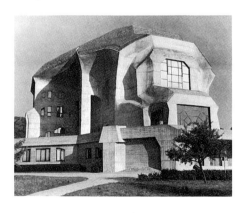

clumsy. Contemporaries praised the beautiful effect of the light falling through the great screen of material, and supplemented by light sources behind tinted glass insets in the upper part of the walls. It may also be that the dark panelling created an intimate atmosphere similar to that said to have been achieved in the recently completed Stuttgart Hoftheater by Heilmann and Littmann, but despite this, the interior only half-fulfilled the promise of the early designs. The exhibition was forced to close early by the outbreak of war, and this prevented thorough testing of the tripartite stage, an idea which was not resurrected.

In designing this theatre van de Velde had once more traversed his entire career, moving from a talented, dilettante beginning to ultimate mastery. The unacademic design of this building was a clear demonstration of his progress: it had not come into being 'despite everything' – against all resistance, as it were – but rather had been made possible by unusual requirements. The Cologne Werkbund theatre was architecture of a kind that a trained architect practising exclusively in that field could not have produced successfully. The musicality of the building derives from an unusually broad sensibility, able to translate complex education and sophisticated knowledge into appropriate form.

It is clear that this was a starting-point from which further progress could be made. Nothing followed directly – it appears that van de Velde himself was unaware of the extent of his achievement – but in 1927 he built La Nouvelle Maison

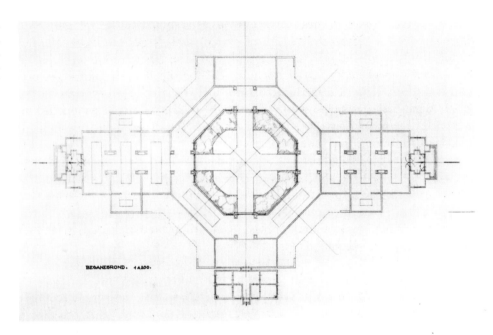

BEGANEGROND. 1 A 200.

in Tervuren near Brussels for himself. Between the two came the war, exile in Holland and his desperate attempt to find salvation in monumental art. This detour and twelve years of procrastination were certainly caused to some extent by van de Velde's disbelief that, because of the abrupt, although possibly anticipated, end to which his life in Germany had come, this particular period of his working life could produce any definite results. The times must have seemed fragmented and tragically incomplete to him. Finally, because he had been pursuing entirely different ends from those he had just achieved, he was hardly in a position correctly to assess the view of architecture expressed in the Cologne theatre. There seemed to be no way forward from here.

It was not until a new generation began to make its presence felt in the mid-1920s that van de Velde discovered he was its precursor, and that he had much in common with the ideas of younger artists. Finally the vision which had floated before him for so long, but which had hitherto eluded his grasp, took shape. Architecture focused on the external shell of a building was now gaining acceptance; it was emphatically substantial and drew its effect from the power of vol-

Preliminary ground plan for the Rijksmuseum Kröller-Müller in Otterlo, 1935; the articulation corresponds largely with the final version

ume. The outer casing of these buildings was thus similar to the 'wet garments' worn by Greek statues – it revealed the organic presence of the architecture by supple modulation, rather than concealing it. In the sphere of architecture this procedure was decidedly anti-classical; it renounced canons of traditional form and devoted itself to a directly functional idea. Of all the younger architects, Erich Mendelsohn was closest to van de Velde; their dynamic ideas touched directly. The Einstein Tower (1917–21) continued the ideas behind the Cologne theatre in individual form and the Universum cinema in Berlin (1926) was a new high point in the development of the architecture for which van de Velde had sounded the first notes. (In the same way as in Cologne, and apparently on the basis of related laws, the exterior was superior to the interior in these cases as well.) Rudolf Steiner's second Goetheanum (1924–28), however, for which van de Velde's theatre was presumably a model, at best proved how crudely the concept had been misunderstood in Dornach.

An affinity with that variety of the modern represented by Erich Mendelsohn in the mid-1920s can be seen in almost all the buildings for which van de Velde was responsible after his return to Belgium. Faith in taut but simple form is a constant feature, with features added to accentuate, and to broaden the general

Rijksmuseum Kröller-Müller in Otterlo, view of the sequence of galleries around the inner courtyard, 1938

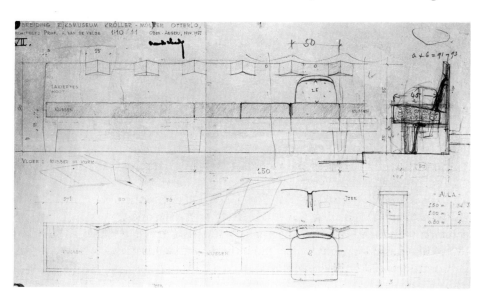

Drawing for the seating in the extended Rijksmuseum Kröller-Müller in Otterlo with corrections by Henry van de Velde, dating from 1952

Groot Haesebroek house in Wassenaar/Holland, 1930

conception of the avant-garde and avoid a doctrinaire position. At the same time these individual traits can be traced from van de Velde's previous work, and there is continuity of artistic style throughout the entire span of his *œuvre*. At this point it became clear that the lineaments of van de Velde's work had never been decorative in the usual way, but had always expressed the inner force of the object – whether chair or building, item of tableware or door handle.

If we use the later work to explain that which had preceded it – and the Werkbund theatre is a focal point in either direction – then the Kröller-Müller museum, in the much reduced form in which it was finally built from 1937 to 1953, possibly represents yet another step forward. The idea of the ground plan is based on the old designs of 1921 to 1926, but the extraordinary concentration which was finally achieved is only comprehensible as the result of a process which is not only the sum of all that had gone before, but which has managed to filter out all but its quintessential qualities.

Yet again an ornamental figure – this time geometrical and severe – formed the starting-point. One result of its shape, wilful to a certain extent, is the beautiful spatial continuum around the central courtyard. It is possible to see stage by stage how the architecture itself grew from the autonomous ornamental figure during the planning stages. The decisive thrust was given by the resolve to abandon symmetry and move the entrance from the centre to one of the ends. The ornamental effect was lost in this way, but the rhythmic spatial composition, which from the outset had been the aim of the original design, was preserved.

The Kröller-Müller museum in the form in which it was opened in 1938 is probably the most precise building which van de Velde ever designed. Indeterminate features have finally been rooted out, but as before we have movement instead of petrification. This is only true in the interior, however – the most striking feature of the building is the fluent sequence of its rooms. This is enhanced by subtle details like the rounded cladding of the corridor walls.

The polygonal refraction of the lecture theatre, not added until after the Second World War, is directly reminiscent of van de Velde's beginnings – a late after-effect of the ground plan of the Bloemenwerf house. The last drawing checked and signed by van de Velde also shows the idiosyncrasy of creating a particular rhythm by the refraction of forms. The apparently superfluous shaping of the backs of the seats was functionally justified by the wish that each patron should be able to feel where his head touched the seat. Who could resist superfluity of this kind?

Plaster model of the theatre at the Werkbund exhibition in Cologne, 1913

Entrance to the theatre at the Werkbund exhibition in Cologne, 1914

View of the left-hand side façade

The upper foyer

Theatre at the Werkbund Exhibition in Cologne, 1914

Henry van de Velde was always fascinated by theatrical commissions, which obviously reflected his own interests. However, in 1904 plans to build a summer theatre in Weimar came to nothing (pages 85 and 89) and the Théâtre des Champs-Elysées in Paris was taken out of his hands (1910/11, pages 158–61). Between these two events his attempt to take part in a competition for a theatre in Lübeck also came to nothing. The Cologne project was the first to be realized.

The building combined in surprisingly mature form the fundamental tendencies which had shaped the artist's œuvre until now. The most distinctive feature was the articulation of the building, which made the exterior a precise expression of the interior. The sequence of foyer, auditorium and stage, with associated side passages and offstage areas, had been opened up and could be observed like the components of a car body. This differentiating procedure did not, however, prevent the establishment of overall form, which simply evolved in a different way from usual. In place of a preconceived unified appearance an attempt was made here to develop a composition which differed according to the point from which it was viewed. The building invited the onlooker to move, and thus continued an idea already adumbrated in the architecture of the Hohenhof (pages 136–45). Invidual sections complemented each other to make a many-faceted and multiform overall design. For these intentions to succeed, however, it was essential to bring the elements so close to each other that there was interplay between them. Van de Velde's shaping hand can be detected in the overall articulation as well as the soft flow of outline and transposition.

The supple appearance of this architecture was again close to the best work of van de Velde's early period. There is no fundamental difference between the curved desk of 1899 (page 8) and the theatre designed fifteen years later in 1914. Both show in related fashion physical differentiation and linear dynamics.

The unusually low façade of the theatre was so designed because the site included an embankment. The exhibition centre was on the bank of the Rhine, and had to be suitably protected. This meant that the entrance was raised, while the auditorium and stage were at ground level. This limitation finally proved an advantage both for the outward appearance of the building and for the organization of its interior. Theatre-goers entered the building at the level of the highest row of seats and followed the internal movement of the auditorium as they went down the steps. The division of the foyer into individual sections had been developed in a way which was extraordinarily clear, full of nuance and harmonious – van de Velde had hit on one of his best ground plan designs for the theatre.

Entrance side above the embankment

Right-hand side façade seen from the level of the embankment

Auditorium

View of the stage

Theatre at the Werkbund Exhibition in Cologne, 1914

The Cologne building included the first example of a stage divided into three, a notion which van de Velde considered to be his particular contribution to the development of the theatre. On each side of the stage, set at a slight angle, were two side acting areas, which could be used alternately. It was also possible to use all three areas at once, creating a panoramic effect. This revolutionary idea was, however, limited to the stage design, and had no effect on the shape of the auditorium; the latter's severe contours contrasted with the broken line of the stage. The furnishings also made a surprisingly rigid and ponderous impression. The large central lamp was the focus of the room, contradicting its direct connection with the stage. The solid, semi-circular horizon was one of the elements expected from a modern theatre.

The outbreak of war ended the Werkbund exhibition earlier than had been planned, and restricted the number of performances in the theatre, which had never been intended to be permanent and was pulled down in 1920; van de Velde was unable to repeat the experiment of a stage divided into three. The sculptural decoration in the two façade windows – also something which could have been left out – was by Hermann Obrist. This artist was probably involved because the exhibition directors were particularly committed to him.

The right-hand side foyer

Rear view of the right-hand side of the theatre façade

Continuity

The Werkbund theatre was of central significance in more than one way. Van de Velde's best building to date, it also marked the end of his work in Germany, which was broken off by the war. Thus his working life was interrupted at the point at which it had made its greatest impact, and potential future developments were left in the air. The Cologne theatre was not just the quintessence of everything which preceded it, it also provided a view of a new architecture. Its shell design followed the logic of showing only the volume necessary to contain the space required; this was a rejection of traditional ideas, according to which interior arrangements had to be governed by external rules, an approach all too clearly demonstrated by some neoclassical buildings at the Werkbund exhibition. Van de Velde's theatre was a flexible design set amongst numerous buildings which were specimens of a petrified modernity.

Van de Velde was not able to build on this achievement until twelve years later, when he returned to work in Belgium after his period in Holland. The buildings in this last phase of his working life returned very logically to the principles developed in Cologne and were indeed their continuation. It is therefore possible to see a continuous thread in van de Velde's work and approach extending from 1900 to the classic modern period around 1930. The break generally seen in his contemporaries' work between these two dates did not occur in his case. In design terms the latter phase can be seen to develop from the former.

The outward signs of this are spatial graduation, soft transitions and the emphasis of horizontal elements by cornices and canopies. These can be seen in both the Cologne theatre and the house in Brussels. In both cases monolithic design is replaced by considered composition.

Entrance side of the Wolfers house in Brussels, 1930

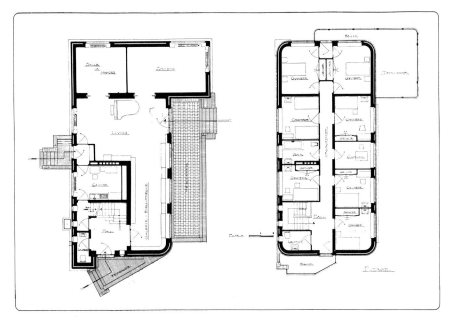

La Nouvelle Maison in Tervuren, 1927

The fourth house Henry van de Velde built for himself showed the extent to which he had succeeded despite regressions in developing specific ideas of form and function. At first glance the markedly stereometric design of the house fits in clearly with the avant-garde notions of the 1920s, but this impression is also fundamentally complemented and extended by the detail. The architecture is not content with the purity demanded by primary forms, but again seeks to enliven the material. Apparently superfluous elements create movement, setting dynamic form against the introversion of the untouched white cube.

This begins with the protruding sections of the roof and proceeds via the rounded corners to the indentation at the base of the bay. The ground plan of the principal storey is essentially severe, but surprisingly rich within the arrangement. The long 'approach' to the central point formed by the living-room could seem superfluous, but harmonizes agreeably with the centre of the house – an effect which cannot be shown on a photograph. The informal generosity which was such a strong feature of Hohe Pappeln (page 132) is repeated here.

Garden side of the house

◁ Entrance side, living-room and ground plans of the two main storeys

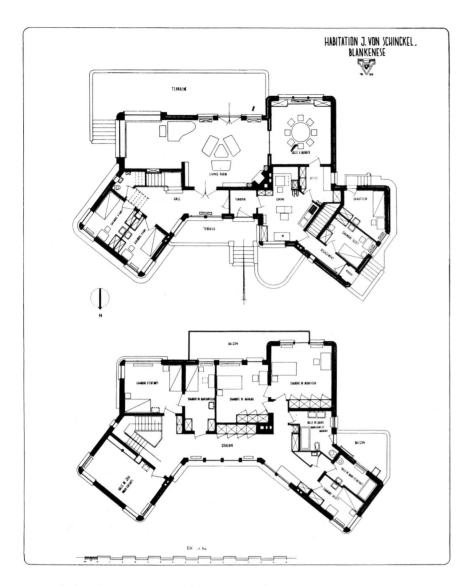

Ground plans for the Schinckel house in Hamburg, 1926

Entrance side of the Schinckel house in Hamburg, 1926

Various Private Houses, 1926–32

In 1926 Henry van de Velde built a villa for his son-in-law in which the double break in the ground plan is clearly reminiscent of pre-war notions and at the same time a perfect example of the use of points where parts of the building intersect for purposes of articulation. The double L-shape made it possible to place the main façade (page 106) parallel with the River Elbe and at the same time to take up the lines of the streets.

The little outpatients' clinic is also sensitively set at a junction where two streets meet not quite at right angles. The curve of the corner liberally mirrors the situation, while the two bays are gently opposed to it. Despite its small scale the building has a number of formal refinements: the soft moulding of the left bay, for example, and the design of the roof cornice.

The artifically created run of windows in the upper storey of the Martens villa is a left-over from the vocabulary of the 1920s which van de Velde belatedly adopted here in curiously uncontrolled fashion.

Dr Martens's villa in Astene/Belgium, 1932

Dr Martens's clinic in Astene/Belgium, 1932

One of the two staircases

Detail of the south side

Old People's Home in Hanover, 1929

The building was commissioned by a foundation, and its stately appearance suggests that the intention was to run it along the lines of a sanatorium.

The design approximates that of buildings of the immediate pre- and post-war years, and is probably closest to the museum for the Kröller-Müller collection (page 172).

The detailed treatment is of great superiority and maturity, however, and the many facets and layers of the garden façade make a subtle effect which is never hard, despite great precision. The three-dimensional pattern of the polygonal bays is relieved and cushioned by the broad horizontals of base course and roof – spatial and linear elements work in fascinating symbiosis in this architecture.

The stepped banisters in the interior adopt a motif typical of the period; here it is not isolated, but in harmony with the exterior.

Garden side of the building

Dining-room on the liner *Prince Baudouin*, 1933/34

The *Prince Baudouin*, 1933/34

The Cohen house in Brussels, 1929

Lounge on the liner *Prince Baudouin*, 1933/34

Technical Design

More than thirty years after the collapse of the project for an ocean liner for the German shipbuilder Albert Ballin, van de Velde designed two Belgian mail steamers. His contract included both the exterior and the entire interior. He followed his own view of functionality, whereby light objects were made to look as weightless as possible, but things that had to be heavy – such as furniture bolted to the floor, for example – were made to look extremely heavy indeed. To this extent van de Velde had remained true to himself.

There is no denying that the exterior of the two ships was very elegant, eschewing the usual notions of 'streamlined' design. Designs for Belgian railway carriages and a small German private yacht were also executed during this period – all in all, late fulfilment in a sphere in which he had for so long wanted to work, that of design for a technical purpose.

The Cohen house in Brussels proves that van de Velde continued to aim for architecture that was emphatically functional and akin to the work of an engineer. The façade was conceived like a frame, austere and with a slightly neoclassical look. The spatial structure looks as though it has been applied in layers, or – according to viewpoint – carved out of the heart of the building. The design echoes some very early work – the Esche house in Chemnitz, for example (pages 80 and 81). The photograph shows the house without the slender piers that originally divided the ground-floor windows.

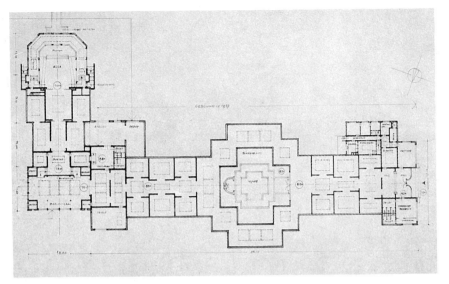

Ground plan with extension

The Kröller-Müller Museum in Otterlo, 1937–53

The idea behind the original design can still just be discerned in the aerial photograph of the building in which the Kröller-Müller collection was finally housed. Two wings with bulbous ends are built on to a square central section (page 172; the break in symmetry caused by the extension on the left did not occur until later and was probably not part of the original design). The building is emphatically plain and seems like a simplified model for the old design. However, where things were originally concealed behind monumental forms, they are now clearly revealed. The architecture is a shell, concealing and directing inwards. For this reason the exterior is not overloaded, but determined by precise organization of mass. A contributory factor here is that the building is placed immediately on the level ground, and the vertical and horizontal meet directly.

The aerial photograph reveals something of the early ornamental design. Seen from above this section seems like a continuation of the routes round the museum which van de Velde drew in the earlier plan.

The wreath-like sequence of rooms around the inner courtyard is arranged in an unconventional way. It was an unusual procedure to fit together rooms with open corners. The result is smooth transitions and surprising graduations. Every second corner is missing – a bonus, as corners are not useful in museums. Van de Velde's marked inclination to make corners more attractive by chamfering them had the added advantage here of opening up the edges.

Once the visitor has walked half-way round the courtyard – of necessity choosing one direction; the other will be the return route – the first sequence of rooms is repeated, leading finally to the second spatial centre, the sculpture gallery. This includes an added effect: the courtyard offers a view of the sky, and the final room looks out over the surrounding area.

This spatial climax is damped down by a further short sequence of small rooms set at right angles to the sculpture gallery, which act as a distraction. No continuation is expected. The tour finally comes to an abrupt and somewhat unmotivated conclusion, as the lecture room at the end of the axis is not part of the museum proper. Presumably this was dictated by problems of this particular interior.

The tower-like corners in the sculpture gallery again represent a particular notion of van de Velde's. In spatial terms they are not compulsory, but they are extremely solid, in order to counterbalance the pellucid architecture. Their function is essentially artistic.

Aerial photograph

Central section of the north façade

Entrance side

The Kröller-Müller Museum in Otterlo, 1937–53

Various plans and perspective drawings, all dated 1925, show that even at that time the idea of a smaller-scale design had been considered. It was intended to replace the original project on a temporary, rather than permanent, basis. These considerations then led to a surprisingly simple distillation of the monumental design, similar in articulation but much more modest in its mass. The entrance would have remained in the central axis. The cramped design and the windows, which seem uncertain in their size and length, make the design look modest and almost like a Nissen hut. The numerous calculations of the exterior proportions strengthen the improvised character of the complex.

The open form of the many chamfered corners is clearly a left-over from the earlier project; otherwise the plan presents to a large extent the ideas realized twelve years later. The most important alteration, only adopted at the last minute, was the transfer of the entrance to the narrow, western side, entirely changing the orientation of the building, which is now based on a single axis, rather than two intersecting ones as originally planned.

This method of internal organization was unusual, as it placed the principal room not recognizably at the beginning, but half-way round the tour. The element of surprise adds tension to the visit, but does not cause confusion, as the situation is clarified by views through the building. The internal drama of the building thus continues the slightly puzzling impression given by the exterior. Moving the entrance made it possible to keep the north side looking extremely impressive.

The essential counterpart to the entrance was missing at first, as the east façade was originally closed and completely without accents. The sculpture gallery added in 1943 corrected this.

The entrance façade can be seen as a simplified variation of the front view of the Werkbund theatre. Although more austere in detail, it is surprisingly close to the theatre in approach and organization. In the interior, movement occurs first from the light and entirely unsolemn entrance hall to the inner courtyard, which is also very light in its effect. All the doorways are open; visitors are never obstructed by doors.

North side of the Kröller-Müller museum, before the entrance was built

Perspective of a preliminary design, 1925

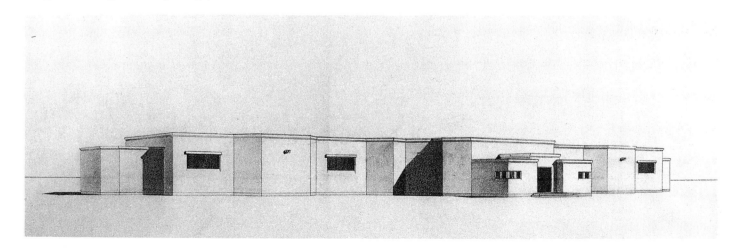

Entrance hall

View through to the inner courtyard

The front central corridor with side picture galleries

Sculpture gallery

List of Illustrations

Where it was necessary to use printed material rather than originals, the following were the principal books used: A. M. Hammacher, *Die Welt Henry van de Veldes*, Cologne, 1967 (referred to as 'Hammacher'); Henry van de Velde, *Geschichte meines Lebens*, Munich, 1962 (referred to as '*Geschichte meines Lebens*'); Karl-Heinz Hüter, *Henry van de Velde, sein Werk bis zum Ende seiner Tätigkeit in Deutschland*, Berlin, 1967 (referred to as 'Hüter'); Karl Ernst Osthaus, *Van de Velde, Leben und Schaffen des Künstlers*, Hagen in Westfalen, 1920 (referred to as 'Osthaus'); *Henry van de Velde, 1863–1957, Persönlichkeit und Werk*, Kunstgewerbemuseum, Zurich, 1958 (referred to as 'Zurich catalogue').

Pictorial material from the archives in Brussels and Otterlo is catalogued according to the classification introduced by Léon Ploegaerts and Pierre Puttemans (*L'Œuvre Architectural de Henry van de Velde*, Brussels, Atelier Volkaerts; Quebec, Presses de l'Université Laval, both 1987). LC/S means La Cambre archive in Brussels/inventory by Klaus-Jürgen Sembach, and RKM/S Rijksmuseum Kröller-Müller in Otterlo/inventory by Klaus-Jürgen Sembach.

Photographs in the La Cambre archive came from Henry van de Velde's own collection and show objects at the time they were created. The collection established by Karl Ernst Osthaus, now administered by the Bildarchiv Foto Marburg, includes mainly photographs which were taken in the years immediately preceding the First World War and thus show the objects a considerable time after they were created. On occasions when Osthaus reproduced older photographs for his own use, the pictures are marked with a 'Z' before the number.

It may be assumed that most of the photographs in the Brussels archive were taken by Louis Held, court photographer in Weimar (LC/S2000–2373, 5000–5375).

Page 8
Desk, 1899, oak with brass fittings, 2.61 m wide; Germanisches Nationalmuseum, Nuremberg, formerly the property of the Berlin publisher Ludwig Löffler; an almost identical model formed part of the interior shown at the Munich Secession exhibition in 1899 (see page 53); photo Sophie Renate Gnamm, Munich.

Page 9
Woodcut, *c.* 1895; from *Dekorative Kunst* III, 1898/99, page 9.

Page 10
Wallpaper, 1895 (see entry under page 22); from *Dekorative Kunst* III, 1898/9, preceding page 1.
Belt buckle, before 1900, silver with amethyst, 9.7 cm wide, now in the Karl-Ernst-Osthaus-Museum, Hagen; photo Kunstgewerbemuseum, Zurich.

Page 11
Editor's office for the Paris periodical *L'Art décoratif*, probably 1898; the German magazine *Dekorative Kunst* also appeared in a French edition for a few years; in the background is the picture *Le Chahut* by Georges Seurat (1889/90), later acquired for the Kröller-Müller collection (see pages 208ff.); the fire-screen is identical to the one on page 58; from *Dekorative Kunst* III, 1898/99, page 25.
Packaging design, *c.* 1900; from *Geschichte meines Lebens*, page 141.

Page 12
Sun on the Sea, 1888/89, black chalk on grey paper, 23 × 31.5 cm, entitled *Synthèse rythmique* on rear; formerly in the Nele van de Velde collection; from 'Hammacher', page 52.
Still-life with Fruit Bowl, Pots and Cutlery, 1886, oil on canvas, 92 × 75 cm, signed bottom right 'van de Velde 86'; Rijksmuseum Kröller-Müller, Otterlo; from 'Hammacher', page 117.

Page 13
Henry van de Velde, *c.* 1890; from *Cahiers Henry van de Velde*, 12–13, Brussels, 1974, page 13.

Page 14
Blankenberghe, 1888, oil on canvas, 71 × 100 cm; Kunsthaus, Zurich; photograph by the museum.

Page 15
Garden in Kalmthout, probably 1892, oil on canvas, 70 × 94.6 cm; Bayerische Staatsgemäldesammlung, Neue Pinakothek, Munich; photograph Blauel-Gnamm, Artothek.
Title vignette for the magazine *Van Nu en Straks*, 1893; woodcut, 12.5 × 18 cm.

Pages 16 and 17
Three vignettes for the magazine *Van Nu en Straks*, 1893; reproduced in approximately the original size.

Page 18
Abstract Plant Composition, 1892/93, pastel, 47 × 49 cm; Rijksmuseum Kröller-Müller, Otterlo; photograph Tom Haartsen, Ouderkerk.
Dunescape with Sea, 1892/93, pastel on pink paper, 24 × 31 cm; Bibliothèque Royale, Brussels; photograph by the museum.

Page 19
Angel Watch, 1893, tapestry in appliqué embroidery, wool on linen, outlines in silk thread, 140 × 233 cm; Kunstgewerbemuseum, Zurich; photograph by the museum.
Reaper, probably late 1891 or early 1892, limewater colour on canvas, 75 × 95 cm; formerly in Thyl van de Velde's collection; from 'Hammacher', page 59.

Page 20
The Folkwang-Museum in Hagen, exterior, designed by the Berlin architect C. Gérard and built in 1899; from August Hoff *et al.*, *Karl Ernst Osthaus, Leben und Werk*, Recklinghausen, 1971, page 125.
Showcase in the upper hall of the Folkwang-Museum in Hagen, 1901; photograph Marburg 1.032956.

Page 21
Picture gallery in the upper storey of the Folkwang-Museum in Hagen, 1901; centre is the figure *The Bronze Age* by Auguste Rodin; photograph Marburg 618898.

Entrance hall of the Folkwang-Museum with Georges Minne's *Fountain with Boys*, 1901; from August Hoff *et al.*, *Karl Ernst Osthaus, Leben und Werk*, Recklinghausen, 1971, page 131.

Page 22
Wallpaper, 1895, often used in van de Velde's early interiors (see also pages 45 and 53), also in other colour combinations in the La Cambre archive; from *Dekorative Kunst* III, 1898/99, preceding page 1.
Poster for the Tropon factory, Cologne-Mülheim, 1897, lithograph, published as a supplement to the magazine *Pan*, issue 4; Museum für Kunst und Gewerbe, Hamburg; photograph by the museum.

Page 23
Bedroom and dining-room in the Hohenhof in Hagen, 1907/8, recently reconstructed (see also page 143); photographs Klaus Frahm, Hamburg.

Page 24
Dining-room for theatre director Curt von Mutzenbecher in Wiesbaden, probably 1906; whereabouts unknown; from *Kunst und Künstler* V, 1906/7, page 56.

Page 25
Dining-room, shown at the 'Kunstgewerbe' exhibition in Dresden, 1906; the room was bought at the time by the industrialist Paul Schulenburg and later installed in his villa in Gera (see page 166); from *Kunst und Künstler* V, 1906/7, page 48.

Page 26
Entrance to Theodor Springmann's villa in Hagen, 1914/15 (see also page 167); photograph Marburg 626154.

Page 27
Reception room in the Dürckheim villa in Weimar, 1912; state unknown; photograph Marburg 606231.
Rest room at the 'Kunstgewerbe' exhibition in Dresden, 1897; the room before it was finally decorated with large plants and items from the exhibition; photograph Marburg Z.25081.

Page 28
Ceiling light fitting, *c.* 1905; constructed by Otto Bergner, art metalworker to the court; Berka/Thuringia; from *Innendekoration* XVII, 1906, page 80.

Page 29
Ceiling light fitting, *c.* 1905; constructed by Otto Bergner, art metalworker to the court; Berka/Thuringia; from *Innendekoration* XVII, 1906, page 81.

Page 30
Cover design for Friedrich Nietzsche's *Ecce Homo*, 1908; photograph Marburg 618918.

Page 31
Henry van de Velde in Oberägeri/Switzerland, the last place in which he lived, 1957; he is wearing a zipped suit of his own design; photograph by Klaus-Jürgen Sembach.

Page 32
Henry van de Velde with Frau Esche at the upper garden gate of her villa in Chemnitz, probably 1903; personal photograph.
Opening of the 'Künstlerbund' exhibition in the Grossherzogliches Museum in Weimar on 1 July 1906; from left to right: Harry Graf Kessler, Ludwig von Hofmann, Max Klinger, Henry van de Velde, Theodor Hagen and Karl Olde; photograph by Louis Held, Weimar, who also photographed most of Henry van de Velde's work.

Page 33
Maria van de Velde with her children in Weimar, c. 1905; the picture is by Louis Held, Weimar.
Henry van de Velde, probably c. 1900 in his Berlin period; photographer unknown.

Page 34
Henry van de Velde in the workshops of the Société anonyme van de Velde in Ixelles near Brussels, probably 1897; the address was 53 rue Gray; in the foreground on the left is the cupboard featured on page 79; from 'Hammacher', page 98.

Page 36
Maria Sèthe, painted by Théo van Rysselberghe, 1891; Koninklijk Museum voor Schone Kunsten, Antwerp; photo by the museum.
Philip Webb, Red House in Bexleyheath/Kent, built for William Morris in 1859.
The Bloemenwerf house in Uccle near Brussels, 1895; photograph by Carla de Benedetti, Milan, c. 1960.

Page 37
Garden side of the Leuring house in Scheveningen, 1902; photograph Marburg 1.064457.
Henry van de Velde on the stairs of the Bloemenwerf house, between 1895 and 1900; from Geschichte meines Lebens, plate 40.
The third house Henry van de Velde built for himself, De Tent in Wassenaar, Holland, 1920/21; pulled down in 1961; photograph La Cambre LC/S 2124.

Page 38
Maria van de Velde in the hall of the Bloemenwerf house; she is wearing one of the reform dresses which Henry van de Velde designed in large numbers at the time; in the background is her portrait by Théo van Rysselberghe, on the piano a score by Richard Wagner; between 1895 and 1900; from Dekorative Kunst VII, 1901, page 35.
Dining-room, exhibited in the 'Salon Art Nouveau' in Paris, December 1895 (see page 55); from Geschichte meines Lebens, plate 25.

Page 39
House of Mme Sèthe, Henry van de Velde's mother-in-law, presumably built shortly after the Bloemenwerf house, which is close by; later extended, but its essential detail has survived; photo Marburg Z.25074.

Page 40
Holiday villa in Wartenberg, Bavaria, built by Henry van de Velde for the Weimar sculptor Richard Engelmann in 1913; it is still standing today; personal photograph.

Advertisement for Henry van de Velde's firm in L'Art décoratif, 1898; apparently the address was the Bloemenwerf house in Uccle and not the workshop in Ixelles; from Dekorative Kunst III, 1898/99.

Page 41
The Bloemenwerf house in Uccle near Brussels, 1895; on the left is the bay window of the dining-room, on the right the kitchen door; the house has scarcely been altered at all; from 'Hammacher', page 79.

Page 42
Drawings with watercolour of the front and rear of the Bloemenwerf house in Uccle near Brussels in 1895; the drawings correspond to what was finally built, though the central section of the back was later raised; formerly in the collection of Thyl van de Velde, Brussels; photographs Kunstgewerbemuseum, Zurich.

Page 43
The Bloemenwerf house in Uccle near Brussels, 1895, photographed several years after it was built (probably c. 1910); photograph Marburg 681063.
Sketch plan of the ground floor of the Bloemenwerf house in Uccle near Brussels, 1895, drawing with watercolour, with numerous pencilled notes; largely in accordance with what was built; formerly in the collection of Thyl van de Velde, Brussels; photograph Kunstgewerbemuseum, Zurich.

Page 44
Chairs from the dining-room of the Bloemenwerf house in Uccle near Brussels, 1895; ash with straw seats, height of centre chair 93 cm; Kunstgewerbemuseum, Zurich; photograph Sophie Renate Gnamm, Munich.

Page 45
Study on the gallery above the entrance to the Bloemenwerf house in Uccle near Brussels, overlooking the central two-storey hall on the right; in the background a printing press and the Divan Japonais poster (Henri de Toulouse-Lautrec, 1892); on the left-hand easel an abstract painting (probably by Henry van de Velde); top right on the shelf a photograph of the Dutch painter Johan Thorn-Prikker, with whom Henry van de Velde worked on several occasions between 1895 and 1900; for the wallpaper see page 22; from Geschichte meines Lebens, plate 36; photograph Charles Lefébure, Brussels.
The large drawing office on the ground floor of the Bloemenwerf house in Uccle near Brussels; on the right Maria van de Velde with a piece of embroidery of the kind used by Henry van de Velde to decorate reform clothes; on the wall is the same (or a very similar) abstract to the one upstairs in the gallery, directly by the window the Abstract Plant Composition (1892/93, see page 18), but upside-down; between 1895 and 1900; photo from the Henry-van-de-Velde-Gesellschaft collection in Hagen.

Page 46
Henry van de Velde in his first home in Weimar, 11 Cranachstrasse, where he lived from 1902 to 1906; the cupboard had already appeared in his Berlin home (an almost identical version is to

be found in the Badisches Landesmuseum, Karlsruhe); for the sofa in the room behind see page 87; the portrait bust of van de Velde is by Constantin Meunier; photograph La Cambre LC/S 2280.

Page 47
Woodcut for the title page of the volume of poetry Salutations dont d'angéliques by Max Elskamp, 1893; the Belgian poet was a boyhood friend of van de Velde; from Geschichte meines Lebens, page 57.

Page 48
The Eiffel Tower in Paris, 1889.

Page 49
Chair from the Bloemenwerf house, 1895; photograph Sophie Renate Gnamm, Munich.

Page 50
Title vignette for the volume Dominical by Max Elskamp, 1892; from Dekorative Kunst III, 1898/99, page 9.

Page 51
Armchair, padouk wood with batik cover, 1898; Nordenfjelske Kunstindustrimuseum, Trondheim; sewing table with swing drawer, c. 1905; Museum für Kunsthandwerk, Frankfurt/Main; photograph Kunstgewerbemuseum, Zurich.

Page 52
Vignette; the flow of its lines seems to reflect that of the desk on page 53; from Dekorative Kunst III, 1898/99, page 1.

Page 53
Study, shown at the Secession exhibition in Munich, 1899; for the desk see page 8, for the document cupboard page 79 and for the wallpaper page 22; photograph Marburg 1.009040.

Page 54
Angel Watch, 1893, tapestry (for further details see notes to page 19); Kunstgewerbemuseum, Zurich; photograph by the museum.

Page 55
Smoking-room in mahogany, exhibited at the 'Salon Art Nouveau' in Paris, 22 rue de Provence, opened by Samuel Bing, a specialist in the art of eastern Asia, at Christmas 1895 (see also page 38); frieze and mosaic were by the Belgian artist Georges Lemmen; from Dekorative Kunst III, 1898/99, page 19.
Interior for Léon Biart in Brussels, 1896/97; photograph Marburg Z.25083. (When the picture was published in Dekorative Kunst III, 1898/99, the Morris design in the upper section of the room had been removed.)

Page 56
Poster for the Tropon factory, Cologne-Mülheim, 1897 (for further details see notes to page 22); Museum für Kunst und Gewerbe, Hamburg; photo by the museum.

Page 57
Sale-room for the Havana Company in Berlin, Mohrenstrasse 11/12, 1899; no longer in existence; photo Marburg Z.25066.
Reform dress, worn by Frau Salomonsohn, whose husband was later to commission work

from van de Velde; the photograph was taken *c.* 1900 in Henry van de Velde's Berlin home; on the wall is the abstract shown on page 45; from *Deutsche Kunst und Dekoration* X, 1902, page 379.

Page 58
Part of the reading-room in Bruno and Paul Cassirer's art gallery in Berlin, 35 Victoria-strasse, 1898; from *Dekorative Kunst* III, 1898/99, page 225.
Memorial plinth for the Belgian freedom fighter Frédéric de Mérode, Place des Martyrs, Brussels, 1898; figure and plaque are by the Belgian sculptor Paul du Bois, who was van de Velde's brother-in-law; photograph Marburg 617345.

Page 59
Candlestick, 1902; silvered bronze, 28 cm high; Württembergisches Landesmuseum, Stuttgart; photo by the museum.

Page 60
Candelabrum, 1902, silvered bronze, 59 cm high; Nordenfjelske Kunstindustrimuseum, Trondheim; photograph Kunstgewerbe-museum, Zurich.

Page 61
Salon for François Haby, court hairdresser in Berlin, 7 Mittelstrasse, 1901; the picture shows the interior without the later alterations (cf. 'Osthaus', page 29); surviving material in various museums in the GDR; from *Dekorative Kunst* VIII, 1901, page 490.

Page 62
Showcase in the picture gallery of the Folkwang-Museum in Hagen, 1901. There was a showcase like this in each of the four corners of the room, now no longer in existence; contemporary critics found fault with the contradictory juxtaposition of stone (base) on wood (floor); photograph Marburg 618900.

Page 63
Items from a Meissen porcelain service, *c.* 1905: teacup, coffee-cup, teapot, dinner plate, sugar basin and milk jug, decoration in gold, occasionally also blue; the service was produced in a limited edition; individual items in various German museums; photograph Marburg 618772.
Items from a set of silver cutlery, 1903: spoon for fruit sauces, fruit knife and fork, ice-cream spoon, fish knife and fork; made in a limited edition by the court jeweller Theodor Müller in Weimar; individual items in various German museums; photograph Sophie Renate Gnamm, Munich.

Page 64
Silver jardinière, 1902, part of an extensive table set, a present from Thuringia to the grand-ducal couple; whereabouts unknown; photograph La Cambre LC/S 2289.
Two basketwork chairs, *c.* 1905; manufactured by the firm of August Bosse, Weimar; from *Innendekoration* XVII, 1906, page 77.

Page 65
Silver tea service with boxwood handles, 1905, made in a limited edition by court jeweller Theodor Müller in Weimar; length of tray 49.2 cm; Karl-Ernst-Osthaus-Museum, Hagen; photograph Kunstgewerbemuseum, Zurich.

Page 66
Silver candelabrum, probably 1907; privately owned; photograph Kunstgewerbemuseum, Zurich.

Page 67
Museum hall at the 'Kunstgewerbe' exhibition in Dresden, 1906; on the right is a view of a smoking-room designed by Henry van de Velde with frescos by Maurice Denis; the brass fittings must have toned well with the pictures, which are largely in shades of blue and green (paintings now in the Thüringisches Landes-museum in Weimar; remainder no longer in existence); from H. Pudor. *Dokumente des Modernen Kunstgewerbes*. Series C, Leipzig, no date, page 84.
In the museum hall in Dresden, 1906; photograph Marburg 1.027881.

Page 68
Machine room for the Harkort Company in Hagen, 1904; the precise site is no longer known, probably no longer in existence; photograph Marburg Z.29803.

Page 69
Door furniture for the Nietzsche archive in Weimar, 1903; still at the original site; photograph Marburg Z.25075.

Page 70
Chair, 1898, walnut with ribbed material, 103.5 cm high; Hessisches Landesmuseum, Darmstadt; photographs (on pages 70 and 71) Sophie Renate Gnamm, Munich.

Page 71
Corner sofa in the offices of Dr Wittern, a Lübeck barrister, 1902; whereabouts unknown; from *Innendekoration* XIV, 1903, page 255.
Chair, 1898; see entry for page 70 for details.

Page 72
Capital and staircase in the Folkwang-Museum in Hagen, 1901; they have survived unaltered; photographs Marburg 615129 and 620393.

Page 73
Stair-well in the Folkwang-Museum in Hagen, 1901; it has survived to a large extent; from *Innendekoration* XIII, 1902, page 260.

Page 74
Ceiling aperture and skylight in the Folkwang-Museum in Hagen, 1901; glass colours: pink, green, yellow and violet; no longer in existence; from *Innendekoration* XIII, 1902, page 266.
Silver belt buckle, before 1900, formerly the property of Gertrud Osthaus; Die Neue Sammlung, Munich; photograph Kunstgewerbe-museum, Zurich.

Page 75
Upper hall of the Folkwang-Museum in Hagen, 1901; fittings no longer in existence, railing reconstructed a few years ago from old photographs; from *Dekorative Kunst* XI, 1903, page 15.

Page 76
Music room in the Folkwang-Museum in Hagen, 1901; all wooden parts natural oak, upholstery pink-brown velvet, walls pink-yellow; no longer in existence; from *Innendekoration* XIII, 1902, page 283.

Page 77
Handles on the main door of the Folkwang-Museum in Hagen, 1901; still on the same site; photograph Marburg 619330.

Page 78
Design for a museum of applied art in the Karlsplatz in Weimar, 1903/4; all ground plans, cross-sections and elevations for the project were completed, but it was never built; the Finn Sigurd Frosterus (1876–1956) was involved. Frosterus, who stayed in Weimar on several occasions between 1903 and 1905, was a qualified architect and certainly had some influence on van de Velde, who was self-taught; plan La Cambre, LC/S 4390; photograph Kunstgewer-bemuseum, Zurich.

Page 79
Document cupboard, 1899, oak, 177 cm wide; this piece of furniture originally belonged to a collection designed for the Secession exhibition in Munich in 1899 (see page 53); Germanisches Nationalmuseum, Nuremberg; photograph Sophie Renate Gnamm, Munich.
Cupboard, 1897, 160 cm high; Nordenfjeldske Kunstindustrimuseum, Trondheim; photograph Kunstgewerbemuseum, Zurich.

Page 80
Herbert Esche's house in Chemnitz, 1902/3, shortly after it was built, without the raised section on the left which was added in 1911; it has survived almost unchanged; photograph La Cambre LC/S 2250.
Counters in the Deutsche Bank in Augsburg, 1902; no longer in existence; photograph Marburg Z.25067.

Page 81
Street side of Herbert Esche's house in Chemnitz, 1902/3; the main entrance was behind the arch in the central gable, side rooms on the right; photograph La Cambre, LC/S 2249.
Wardrobe, 1903; from *Innendekoration* XIV, 1903, page 263.

Page 82
In the music room of Herbert Esche's house in Chemnitz, 1902/3; the room was laid out symmetrically on the diagonal, the wall fittings were repeated in mirror image; some of the furniture has survived; photograph Marburg 619469.

Page 83
Design for a building for the Berlin Secession, 1904. There were only minor rooms at the front, behind them was a large windowless hall with top lighting; Sigurd Frosterus was also involved with this design, which was never realized; plan La Cambre LC/S 1500.
Rocking chair, 1904, mahogany with leather upholstery, 100 cm high; Museum für Kunst-handwerk, Frankfurt am Main; photograph Kunstgewerbemuseum, Zurich.

Page 143
Dining-room in the Hohenhof; now in its original state with red wall fabric (lamp reconstructed); photograph Marburg 618853.
One of the two sideboards in the Hohenhof dining-room; on the right is the opening to the conservatory; photograph Marburg 618854.

Page 144
Drawing-room in the Hohenhof; whereabouts of furniture unknown, the Vuillard picture has been replaced by a copy; photograph Marburg 615236.

Page 145
Hohenhof, left-hand section of the conservatory, outside the study; photograph La Cambre LC/S 2187.

Page 146
Pergola on the south side of Rudolf Springmann's house in Hagen, 1910/11; photograph La Cambre LC/S 2200.

Page 147
Street side of Rudolf Springmann's house in Hagen; the villa has been little altered; the bay was originally two storeys high inside, but a ceiling was put in shortly after the house was built; photograph La Cambre LC/S 2228.

Page 148
Henry van de Velde in front of his monument to the physicist and social politician Ernst Abbe in Jena, probably 1911; photograph Marburg 606852.

Page 150
Silver service (c. 1910), an example of the tendency to the monumental in van de Velde's later applied-art work; Karl-Ernst-Osthaus-Museum, Hagen; photograph Marburg 619457.
The Henneberg (1913) and Dürckheim (1912) villas in Weimar; the exteriors have recently been restored, or were distorted to a large extent by early additions; photographs Marburg 606217 and 606224.
Model of the Groot Haesebroek house, 1921, designed for the Kröller-Müller family in Wassenaar, Holland; it still has features quite similar to those of the pre-war villas, residence and gallery being still joined; the project was not realized until 1930, in much simplified form (see page 192); photograph La Cambre LC/S 2112.

Page 151
Design for the façade of the Théâtre des Champs-Elysées in Paris, 1911; plan La Cambre LC/S 4532.
Ground-plan sketch for the Théâtre des Champs-Elysées, Paris, with open staircases at the side of the stage; on the back is written 'Théâtre Grande salle, 1ère Etude, faite à Weimar 25 Janvier 1911'; the slender supports around the auditorium show that this was a steel construction, later replaced by one in concrete by Auguste Perret; plan La Cambre (no number); photograph Sophie Renate Gnamm, Munich.
Sketch of the interior of the Théâtre des Champs-Elysées, 1911, from 'Hüter', page 197.
Théâtre des Champs-Elysées in Paris, sketch of the façade in the final version by Auguste Perret; from Les Cahiers de l'art moderne, no. 6, 15 September 1913.

Page 152
Théâtre des Champs-Elysées in Paris, ground plans of main auditorium (with foyer) and dress circle (with the second, smaller auditorium) in Henry van de Velde's version, 1910/11, cloakrooms in restricted space and a yard to service the stage; from 'Osthaus', pages 132 and 133.

Page 153
Hendrik Petrus Berlage, two designs for the Hoenderloo museum, 1917; apparently the last of many versions; Rijksmuseum Kröller-Müller, Otterlo (there are also other plans there); photograph by the museum.
King Leopold III's study in the château in Brussels, 1935; anteroom and study separated by a sliding door; on the wall are maps of the Congo and Belgium; present state not known; photograph Bibliothèque Royale, Brussels.
The Belgian Pavilion at the World Fair in Paris, 1937 (Henry van de Velde with J. J. Eggericx and Raphaël Verwilghen); a large complex surrounding an inner courtyard and with a side arm stretching down to the banks of the Seine; from Geschichte meines Lebens, plate 131.
The Belgian Pavilion at the New York World Fair in 1939 (Henry van de Velde with Victor Bourgeois and Léon Stijnen), three wings around a courtyard; rebuilt in different configuration in 1941 in Richmond/Virginia by another architect; from Geschichte meines Lebens, plate 132.

Page 154
Binding for the de luxe edition of Friedrich Nietzsche's Also sprach Zarathustra, 1908; photograph Marburg 619458.
Double-page title vignette for an edition of Friedrich Nietzsche's Ecce Homo, 1908; drawing La Cambre LC/S 1896.

Page 155
Kötschau family tomb in Weimar, 1909; bronze slabs set in stone; now very dilapidated; photograph Marburg Z.25079.

Page 156
Interior of the Abbe memorial in Jena, 1909–11, with bust by Max Klinger and reliefs by Constantin Meunier; the other three sides of the marble plinth are decorated with reliefs in antique style; photograph Marburg 619484.

Page 157
The Abbe memorial in Jena, one of the four identical entrance sides; bronze gates closed off the entrances when necessary; the roof cladding is now different, but otherwise the building has survived in good condition; photograph Marburg 619484.

Page 158
Two early versions of the façade of the Théâtre des Champs-Elysées, Paris, 1910/11; scale 1:50, coloured drawings, the lower signed 'mars 11 v.d.V.'; plans La Cambre LC/S 1516 and 4566.
Middle version of the façade of the Théâtre des Champs-Elysées; scale 1:100, coloured drawing, numbered 'IV' top left; plans La Cambre LC/S 4535.

Page 159
Coloured drawing of the main auditorium of the Théâtre des Champs-Elysées; scale 1:50, signed bottom left 'van de Velde Nov. 10'; plan La Cambre LC/S 1902.
Théâtre des Champs-Elysées, middle version of the façade; scale 1:100, coloured drawing, numbered 'III' top left; plan La Cambre LC/S 4534.

Page 160
Two late versions of the façade of the Théâtre des Champs-Elysées; scale 1:100, pencil drawings, the first numbered 'IX' top right, signed top right '1 juillet 11 v.d.V.', the second numbered 'X' top left; plans La Cambre LC/S 4542 and 4543.
Façade design for the Théâtre des Champs-Elysées, variation of the version on page 161; scale 1:100, drawing in coloured pencil; plan La Cambre LC/S 4538.

Page 161
Perspective of what was probably the final version of the designs for the façade of the Théâtre des Champs-Elysées; pencil drawing, dated 'Paris le 22 mai 1911' bottom left; plan La Cambre LC/S 4539.
Façade design for the Théâtre des Champs-Elysées, variation on the above version; scale 1:100, coloured pencil drawing, numbered 'VIII' top left; plan La Cambre LC/S 4541.

Page 162
Perspective of what was probably the final version of the Nietzsche stadium in Weimar, 1911/12, red chalk drawing; in the background on the left is the U-shaped layout of the stands; plan La Cambre LC/S 1504.
Two preliminary designs for the Nietzsche stadium, red chalk and pencil drawings respectively; plan La Cambre LC/S 1503 and 4521.

Page 163
Nietzsche stadium, version of the temple on a square ground plan, red chalk drawing; plan La Cambre LC/S 1508.
Nietzsche stadium, one side of the spectators' stands; photo La Cambre LC/S 2215.

Page 164
Central hall and staircase of the Körner villa in Chemnitz, 1913; photograph Marburg 619479.

Page 165
Street side of the Körner villa in Chemnitz, 1913; badly damaged in the Second World War and later rebuilt in different form; photograph Marburg 619477.
Ground plans; from 'Hüter', page 139.

Page 166
Garden side of the Schulenburg villa in Gera, 1913/14; on the right is the porter's lodge section, the tower-like structure on the roof provided light for the central hall; the exterior has survived almost unaltered; photograph Marburg 619440.
Porter's lodge of the Schulenburg villa in Gera; photograph Marburg 619442.

Page 167
North-west corner of Theodor Springmann's villa in Hagen, 1914/15; the house was started but not completed during the First World War, and then completed by someone else (see also page 26); destroyed in the Second World War; photograph Marburg 606234.

Page 168
Smoking-room in the Dürckheim villa in Weimar, 1912; on the right is the way through to the hall (see also page 27); not now accessible and probably destroyed; photograph Marburg 606234.

Page 169
Dining-room in the Dürckheim villa in Weimar, 1912; not now accessible and probably destroyed; photograph Marburg 606239.

Page 170
Drawing-room in the Dürckheim villa in Weimar, 1912; the central room in the middle section of the house, on the right the door to the dining-room; the furniture is apparently gilded; not now accessible and probably destroyed; photograph Marburg 606238.

Page 171
Design for a museum in Erfurt, 1913/14; two views of the model and ground plans for the two principal storeys; the project was suggested by the then director of the Erfurt collection and later Reichskunstwart Edwin Redslob, but the war prevented the realization of the project; from 'Osthaus', pages 140 and 141, and 'Hüter', pages 184 and 185.

Page 172
Hoenderloo museum, perspective of an early version, 1921; the basic articulation is already completely planned, in later versions only the details were organized a little more flexibly; dated bottom right: '21.7.21'; plan Rijksmuseum Kröller-Müller RKM/SS 7139.
Hoenderloo museum, ground plans of the two main floors with ornamental lines, c. 1922; other, far simpler, ground plans are extant; plans La Cambre LC/S 1153 and 1154.

Page 173
Design for the entrance of the Hoenderloo museum, signed bottom right: 'F. W. Palm 23.6.23' (Palm was presumably the draughtsman); plan Rijksmuseum Kröller-Müller RKM/S 7172.

Page 174
Picture gallery in the Hoenderloo museum, charcoal and pencil drawing, c. 1923; plan Rijksmuseum Kröller-Müller RKM/S 7116.
Director's office in the Hoenderloo museum, c. 1925; plan Rijksmuseum Kröller-Müller RKM/S 7642.
Central hall in the Hoenderloo museum; photograph La Cambre, no number.

Page 175
Perspective of an inner courtyard in the Hoenderloo museum, probably 1923; one of the four courtyards in the central section intended to provide light for rooms on the ground floor behind it and inner rooms on the upper storey; red chalk drawing on card; plan Rijksmuseum Kröller-Müller RKM/S 7123.

Page 176
One of the two staircases in the Hoenderloo museum, probably 1923; coloured chalk drawing on card, signed bottom right: 'L. Terwen' (presumably the draughtsman); plan Rijksmuseum Kröller-Müller RKM/S 7108.

Page 177
Central picture gallery on the upper floor of the Hoenderloo museum, probably 1923; coloured chalk on card, signed bottom right: 'L. Terwen' (presumably the draughtsman); plan Rijksmuseum Kröller-Müller RKM/S 7111.
Entrance hall with a view of adjacent galleries in the Hoenderloo museum, probably 1923; coloured chalk on card, signed bottom right: 'L. Terwen' (presumably the draughtsman); plan Rijksmuseum Kröller-Müller RKM/S 7110.

Page 178
Project for the left bank of the Schelde in Antwerp, version with double gateway and central tower, 1926; the intention was to build a completely new district, commissioned by a Belgian property company, but the project apparently collapsed because of political difficulties; no plans are extant; photograph La Cambre LC/S 2103.
Photomontage of projected buildings for the left bank of the Schelde in Antwerp, 1926; a combination of drawing (background) and photograph (foreground); photograph Bibliothèque Royale, Brussels.
Whm H. Müller & Co.'s travel agency in Rotterdam, 1924; one of the numerous smaller jobs van de Velde did for Kröller's companies; destroyed; photograph Marburg 1.161431.

Page 179
Project for the left bank of the Schelde in Antwerp, version with central gateway, 1926; photograph La Cambre LC/S 2105.
Project for the left bank of the Schelde in Antwerp, variation on the version with central gateway; photograph La Cambre LC/S 2108.

Page 180
The university library in Ghent, 1936, view of the book tower from the inner courtyard; the planning stages are documented with numerous plans and photos of wooden and plaster models (La Cambre and Eugène Delatte archive in Brussels); from 'Hammacher', page 275.

Page 181
The university library in Ghent, 1936, street side with the book tower; photograph owned by the Henry-van-de-Velde-Gesellschaft, Hagen.

Page 182
Henry van de Velde in the Dutch period, probably 1923; in the background drawings for the Hoenderloo museum; the photograph suggests that Henry van de Velde worked as a draughtsman himself, but only a few sketches by him have survived, the vast majority of the drawings in the Brussels and Otterlo archives being the work of assistants; photograph owned by the Henry-van-de-Velde-Gesellschaft, Hagen.

Page 184
Title vignette for an edition of Friedrich Nietzsche's *Dionysos-Dithyramben*, 1914; from 'Hüter', page 75.
Ground plan for the cinema design for the Deutscher Werkbund's exhibition in Cologne, 1913; plan La Cambre LC/S 4394.
Ground plans of the stalls and gallery for the first version of the theatre at the Werkbund exhibition in Cologne, 1913; plans La Cambre LC/S 4397 and 4402.

Page 185
Layout sketch including extension of the plot of land for the theatre at the Werkbund exhibition in Cologne; dated bottom right: '31.7.1913'; plan La Cambre LC/S 4393.
Ground plan of the stalls in the extended design for the theatre at the Werkbund exhibition in Cologne, 1913; plan La Cambre LC/S 4416.
Front view of the extended version of the theatre at the Werkbund exhibition in Cologne, 1913; plan La Cambre LC/S 4407.

Page 186
Ground plans of the stalls and gallery and front view of the third version of the theatre at the Werkbund exhibition in Cologne, largely based on earlier designs, 1913; plans La Cambre LC/S 4419, 4421, 4424.

Page 187
Theatre for the Werkbund exhibition in Cologne, ground plan for an intermediate phase designed while the sites were being switched; the stage area has clearly been expanded, but auditorium and foyer have been transferred almost unchanged; dated bottom right '7.X.13'; plan La Cambre LC/S 4434.
Perspective and ground plan of the theatre at the Werkbund exhibition in Cologne after resiting; preliminary version of the final plan, 1913; plans La Cambre LC/S 4435 and 4438.

Page 188
Front view of the theatre at the Werkbund exhibition in Cologne, 1914; in the foreground is a figure by Georg Kolbe; photograph Marburg 1.169756.
Ground plan of the final version of the theatre at the Werkbund exhibition in Cologne, 1914; the arrangement of the entrance steps is not quite as built; photograph La Cambre LC/S 2298.
Ways of using the divided stage in the theatre at the Werkbund exhibition in Cologne for a performance of *Faust* mounted by Victor Barnowsky, 1914; photographs La Cambre LC/S 5331 and 5334.

Page 189
Cross-section of the final version of the theatre at the Werkbund exhibition in Cologne, 1914; the high space between the auditorium ceiling and the roof ridge may have been necessary for ventilation purposes, but probably the correspondence between internal and external volume, otherwise respected, has been abandoned here for the sake of an impressive juxtaposition of architectural forms; photograph La Cambre LC/S 2299.

Page 190
Erich Mendelsohn, Einstein Tower in Potsdam, 1917–21.
Ground plan of a preliminary design for the Rijksmuseum Kröller-Müller in Otterlo. This attempts, in much reduced and simplified form, to preserve the idea of the ground plan of the large museum in Hoenderloo, dating from 1925, when work on the monumental version was still in progress; dated top right '1925'; plan Rijksmuseum Kröller-Müller RKM/S 7698 (detail); photograph by the museum.
Rudolf Steiner, second Goetheanum in Dornach, 1924–28.

223

Page 191

Preliminary ground plan for the Rijksmuseum Kröller-Müller in Otterlo; the articulation corresponds largely with the final version; dated bottom right 'December 1935'; entrances on the two narrow sides; the square intermediate elements in the central sequence of rooms had side light; plan Rijksmuseum Kröller-Müller RKM/S 7701; photograph by the museum.

Rijksmuseum Kröller-Müller in Otterlo, view of the sequence of galleries around the inner courtyard, 1938; photograph Carla de Benedetti, Milan.

Drawing for the seating in the extended Rijksmuseum Kröller-Müller in Otterlo with corrections by Henry van de Velde, dated top left and signed 'Ober-Aegeri, Nov. 1952 van de Velde'; plan Rijksmuseum Kröller-Müller RKM/S 7744; photograph by the museum.

Page 192

Groot Haesebroek house in Wassenaar/Holland, 1930; large villa for the Kröller-Müller family; symmetrical garden side with behind a somewhat lower side wing around a small garden court; in very good condition inside and out; from 'Hammacher', page 266.

Plaster model of the theatre at the Werkbund exhibition in Cologne, 1913; the articulation on the front of the body of the auditorium and the approach are slight departures from the version built; photograph La Cambre LC/S 2285.

Page 193

Entrance to the theatre at the Werkbund exhibition in Cologne, 1914; sculptural decoration in the windows and presumably also over the protruding roof by Hermann Obrist; photograph Marburg Z.25071.

Page 194

View of the left-hand side façade of the theatre at the Werkbund exhibition; in front of the building is a statue by Hermann Obrist; the exhibition site was on the Deutz side of the Rhine, with the spires of the cathedral in the background; the building was pulled down in 1920; photograph by a private individual.

The upper foyer in the theatre at the Werkbund exhibition in Cologne, 1914; furniture by Josef Hoffmann, decoration over the bar by Cissy Brentano; from Henry van de Velde, Theatre Designs 1904–1914 (catalogue), Architectural Association, London, 1974, page 54.

Page 195

Entrance side of the theatre at the Werkbund exhibition in Cologne above the embankment, 1914; photograph Marburg Z.25070.

Right-hand side façade of the theatre at the Werkbund exhibition in Cologne seen from the level of the embankment, 1914; the fountain in the foreground is by Hermann Obrist; from Dekorative Kunst, XXII, 1914, page 561.

Page 196

Auditorium of the theatre at the Werkbund exhibition in Cologne, 1914; walls in brown wood, ceiling in the same colour, light shaded with fabric, other light sources in the upper wall; photograph Marburg Z.25072.

View of the stage in the theatre at the Werkbund exhibition in Cologne; from Die Rheinlande, volume 25, 1914, page 269.

Page 197

The right-hand side foyer in the theatre at the Werkbund exhibition in Cologne, 1914; staircase with a relief by Milly Steger and space in front of the doorways into the auditorium with wall paintings by Ludwig von Hofmann (two motifs, repeated); stains on the piers and walls were caused by weather damage which delayed the opening of the theatre; from 'Osthaus', page 130, and photograph Marburg Z.25073.

Page 198

Rear view of the right-hand side façade of the theatre at the Werkbund exhibition in Cologne, 1914; photograph La Cambre LC/S 5295.

Page 199

Entrance side of the Wolfers house in Brussels, 1930; semi-detached town villa on a trapezoid ground plan; it has survived in good condition; from 'Hammacher', page 265.

Page 200

Entrance side, living-room and ground plans of the two main storeys of La Nouvelle Maison in Tervuren near Brussels, 1927; from 'Hammacher', page 268, and La Cité, 'Numéro spécial', Brussels, 1933, pages 32 and 33.

Page 201

Garden side of La Nouvelle Maison in Tervuren near Brussels, 1927; in the foreground is the bay containing Henry van de Velde's study, he lived in the house for almost twenty years; it has survived in good condition; photograph La Cambre LC/S 5373.

Page 202

Ground plans for the Schinckel house in Hamburg-Blankenese, 1926; from La Cité, 'Numéro spécial', Brussels, 1933, page 31.

Entrance side of the Schinckel house in Hamburg-Blankenese, 1926; it was built for Joachim von Schinckel, a son-in-law of Henry van de Velde (see also page 106); the house was altered in barbaric fashion by a new owner in 1964; photograph La Cambre, no number.

Page 203

Dr Martens's villa in Astene/Belgium, 1932; now altered and extended; from 'Hammacher', page 282.

Dr Martens's clinic in Astene/Belgium, 1932; building on a right-angle with entrance at the end of one wing, on the left is the surgery, in the centre the laboratory, open to the waiting-room; it has survived in good condition; from 'Hammacher', page 283.

Page 204

One of the two staircases in the Stift für jüdische Damen in Kirchrode, Hanover, 1929; photograph Atelier Heidersberger, Brunswick.

Detail of the south side of the Stift für jüdische Damen in Kirchrode, Hanover, 1929; from 'Zurich catalogue', page 71.

Page 205

Garden side of the Stift für jüdische Damen in Kirchrode, Hanover, 1929 (Heinemann foundation); the building was used as a barracks for a time and subsequently was beautifully restored; photograph Atelier Heidersberger, Brunswick (c. 1960).

Page 206

Dining-room on the liner Prince Baudouin, 1933/34; photograph La Cambre LC/S 2024.

The Prince Baudouin, 1933/34; from Geschichte meines Lebens, plate 125.

Page 207

The Cohen house in Brussels, 1929; terraced house, now houses the Austrian Embassy; it has survived in good condition; privately owned photograph (c. 1960).

Lounge on the liner Prince Baudouin, 1933/34; from 'Hammacher', page 292.

Page 208

Ground plan of the Rijksmuseum Kröller-Müller, Otterlo, main section built 1937/38; adjacent on the left are the sculpture gallery (1941–44) and the lecture theatre with additional picture galleries (1953); from Herman Teirlinck, Henry van de Velde, Brussels 1959, plate 20.

Aerial photograph of the entire Rijksmuseum Kröller-Müller in Otterlo, 1937–53; photograph Zerophoto Nederland, Rotterdam.

Page 209

Central section of the north façade of the Rijksmuseum Kröller-Müller in Otterlo, 1937/38; the Dutch government was committed to building it after the Kröller-Müller family had offered their valuable collection on permanent loan; a severe new section by the architect W.G. Quist was added 1975–77, a corridor joining the east side by the sculpture gallery links the new pavilion with the old building; photograph Hildegard Heise, Hamburg-Blankenese.

Page 210

Entrance side of the Rijksmuseum Kröller-Müller, 1937/38; photograph Hans Sibbelee, Amsterdam.

Page 211

North side of the Kröller-Müller Museum, 1937/38; from 'Hammacher', page 297.

Perspective of a preliminary design for the so-called emergency museum, planned instead of the large version (Hoenderloo museum); dated top left '1925'; central entrance and blind ends of the two wings; they do not correspond with the ground plan on page 190; plan Rijksmuseum Kröller-Müller RKM/S 7710 (detail).

Page 212

Entrance hall of the Rijksmuseum Kröller-Müller, 1937/38; photograph Hans Sibbelee, Amsterdam.

Page 213

View through to the inner courtyard of the Rijksmuseum Kröller-Müller, 1937/38; photograph Hans Sibbelee, Amsterdam.

Page 214

The front central corridor with side picture galleries in the Rijksmuseum Kröller-Müller, 1937/38; photograph Hans Sibbelee, Amsterdam.

Page 215

Sculpture gallery in the extended Rijksmuseum Kröller-Müller, 1941–44; from 'Zurich catalogue', page 72.

Select Bibliography

The most exhaustive bibliography is undoubtedly the one recently prepared by Léon Ploegaerts and Pierre Puttemans. The only essential material missing is from catalogues for the series of exhibitions 'Der Westdeutsche Impuls. Kunst und Umweltgestaltung im Industriegebiet' (Essen and elsewhere, 1984). The following selection is therefore restricted to the most important publications. For contributions in contemporary periodicals see source information in the List of Illustrations.

Publications on Henry van de Velde

Cahiers Henry van de Velde. Brussels, Association Henry van de Velde, nos 1–12/13, 19–1974 (important individual contributions).

Casabella. 'Numero dedicate ad Henry van de Velde'. Milan, G. Mazzochi, no. 237, 1960.

Casteels, Maurice. *Henry van de Velde.* Brussels, Editions des Cahiers de Belgique, 1932.

Cité (La). 'Numéro spécial consacré à Henry van de Velde, directeur de l'ISAD, à l'occasion du 70ième anniversaire du maître-architecte'. Brussels, Librairie Dietrich, 11th year, nos 5/6, 1933.

Deventer, Salomon van. *Henry van de Velde und seine Bindungen an das Ehepaar Kröller-Müller.* Eschwege, Poeschel & Schulz-Schomburg, privately printed, 1953.

Deventer, Salomon van. *Aus Liebe zur Kunst, Das Museum Kröller-Müller.* Cologne, Verlag M. Dumont Schauberg, 1958.

Hammacher, A. M. *De wereld van Henry van de Velde.* Antwerp, Mercatorfonds, 1967 (translated into German as *Die Welt Henry van de Veldes*, Cologne, Verlag M. Dumont Schauberg; translated into French as *Le Monde de Henry van de Velde*, Paris, Librairie Hachette).

Hüter, Karl-Heinz. 'Henry van de Velde als Künstler und Erzieher bis zum Ende seiner Tätigkeit in Weimar'. Berlin, unpublished dissertation, 1962.

Hüter, Karl-Heinz. *Henry van de Velde, sein Werk bis zum Ende seiner Tätigkeit in Deutschland.* Berlin, Akademie Verlag, 1967.

Lenning, H. F. 'Henry van de Velde, his theories and architecture'. New York University, master's thesis, 1940.

Osthaus, Karl Ernst. *Van de Velde, Leben und Schaffen des Künstlers.* Hagen in Westfalen, Folkwang Verlag, 1920 (Reprint: Berlin, Frölich & Kaufmann, 1984).

Pecher, Wolf D. (edited and adapted by). *Henry van de Velde, Das Gesamtwerk: Gestaltung.* Munich, Factum, 1981, vol. 1.

Ploegaerts, Léon and Puttemans, Pierre. *L'Œuvre Architectural de Henry van de Velde.* Brussels, Atelier Volkaerts, and Quebec, Presses de l'Université Laval, 1987.

Rességuier, Clemens. *Die Schriften Henry van de Veldes*, New York, Delphic Press, 1955.

Scheffler, Karl. *Henry van de Velde, Vier Essays.* Leipzig, Insel Verlag, 1913.

Scheffler, Karl. *Die fetten und die mageren Jahre.* Leipzig/Munich, Paul List Verlag, 1946.

Stamm, Günther. 'Studien zur Architektur und Architekturtheorie Henry van de Veldes'. Dissertation, Göttingen, Georg-August-Universität, 1969.

Teirlinck, Herman. *Henry van de Velde.* Brussels, Editions et Ateliers d'art graphique, Elsevier, 1959.

Exhibition catalogues

Henry van de Velde, 1863–1957, Persönlichkeit und Werk. Kunstgewerbemuseum, Zurich, 6 June to 3 August 1958.

Der junge (Henry) van de Velde und sein Kreis, 1883–1893. Foreword and catalogue text by Herta Hesse-Frielinghaus, Karl-Ernst-Osthaus-Museum, Hagen, 18 October to 22 November 1959.

Henry van de Velde. Weimar 1902–1915. Kunsthalle am Theaterplatz, Weimar, 31 March to 28 April 1963.

Henry van de Velde, Gebrauchsgraphik, Buchgestaltung, Textilentwurf. Karl-Ernst-Osthaus-Museum, Hagen, 6 October to 3 November 1963.

Henry van de Velde zum 100. Geburtstag. Württembergischer Kunstverein, Stuttgart, 19 October to 24 November 1963.

Henry van de Velde. 1863–1957. Palais des Beaux-Arts, Brussels, 13 to 19 December 1963.

Henry van de Velde. 1863–1957. Rijksmuseum Kröller-Müller, Otterlo, 21 March to 24 May 1964.

Henry van de Velde, Theatre Designs 1904–1914. Dennis Sharp (ed.), Architectural Association, London, 1974.

Henry van de Velde. Theaterentwürfe 1904–1914. Travelling exhibition, 1977.

Writings by Henry van de Velde

Velde, Henry van de. *Du Paysan en peinture.* Brussels, Editions de l'Avenir social, 1892.

Velde, Henry van de. *Cours d'arts d'industrie et d'ornementation* (Renaissance des arts décoratifs; Esthétique des arts d'industrie et d'ornementation). Brussels, J. H. Moreau, 1894.

Velde, Henry van de. *Aperçus en vue d'une synthèse d'art.* Brussels, Vve Monnom, 1895.

Velde, Henry van de. *Déblaiement d'art.* Brussels, Vve Monnom, 2nd edition, 1895.

Velde, Henry van de. *William Morris, artisan et socialiste.* Brussels, Editions de l'Avenir social, 1898.

Velde, Henry van de. *Die künstlerische Hebung der Frauentracht.* Lecture by Henry van de Velde, Krefeld, Kramer & Braun, 1900.

Velde, Henry van de. *Die Renaissance im modernen Kunstgewerbe.* Berlin, Verlag Cassirer, 1901.

Velde, Henry van de. *Kunstgewerbliche Laienpredigten.* Leipzig, Verlag Seemann, 1902.

Velde, Henry van de. *Notizen von einer Reise nach Griechenland.* Weimar, D. R. Wagner Sohn, 1905.

Velde, Henry van de. *Der neue Stil.* Lecture by Henry van de Velde, delivered at a meeting of the Verband der Thüringer Gewerbevereine zu Weimar, Weimar, C. Steinert, 1906.

Velde, Henry van de. *Vom neuen Stil* (part 2 of the *Laienpredigten*). Leipzig, Insel Verlag, 1907.

Velde, Henry van de. *Rückkehr zum Biedermeier.* Leipzig, Insel Verlag, 1908.

Velde, Henry van de. *Amo.* Weimar, Cranach Presse, 1909.

Velde, Henry van de. *Essays.* Leipzig, Insel Verlag, 1910.

Velde, Henry van de. *Amo.* French text, Weimar, Cranach Presse, 1915.

Velde, Henry van de. *Les formules de la beauté architectonique moderne.* Weimar, Cranach Presse, 1916–17.

Velde, Henry van de. *Die drei Sünden wider die Schönheit.* Corrected German translation with French original, Zurich, M. Rascher, 1918.

Velde, Henry van de. *Formules d'une esthétique moderne.* Brussels, L'Equerre, 1923.

Velde, Henry van de. *Vie et mort de la colonne.* Brussels, Edition du Scarabée d'Or, 1942.

Velde, Henry van de. *Credo. Amo. Formen.* Wiesbaden, Insel Verlag, 1954 (Insel-Bücherei, volume 3).

Velde, Henry van de. *Zum neuen Stil.* Selections from his writings with an introduction by Hans Curjel. Munich, R. Piper, 1955.

Velde, Henry van de. *Geschichte meines Lebens.* Autobiography, edited and translated by Hans Curjel. Munich, R. Piper, 1962 (New edition with a foreword by Klaus-Jürgen Sembach, 1986).

Index of Names

Index of Architectural Works